D0006400

THE GREATER WEIGHT OF GLORY

Spencer Macleod
South Africa, 2000

ROBIN FARNSWORTH

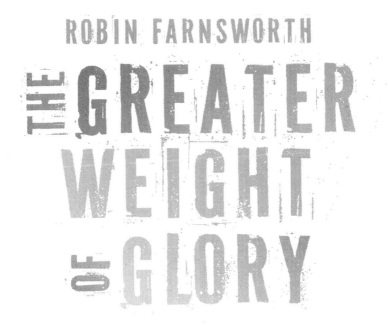

THE GREATER WEIGHT OF GLORY

· A MEMOIR ·

Copyright © 2017 by Robin Farnsworth

ISBN-13: 978-0-69294-554-4

Cover illustration by Robert Lyon

10 9 8 7 6 5 4 3 2 1

All rights reserved. No portion of this book may be reproduced, stored in an electronic retrieval system, or transmitted in any form or by any means—electronic, mechanical, photocopy, recording, or any other—except for brief quotations in printed reviews, without prior permission of the publisher.

Printed in the United States of America

For our light affliction, which is but for a moment,
worketh for us a far more exceeding
and eternal weight of glory.

—2ND CORINTHIANS 4:17 KJV

July 22, 2010

To Jesus,

Let my words bring glory to your name and point others to your saving grace. Let my heart be true and pure and upright; test my motives. I want the courage to speak what You would have me say and the wisdom to keep silent upon those events that You would close the door on forever, to be Yours and mine alone. Let me be content with your Yes and your No and find rest in finishing this race. I love you Lord, more and more. And You, Your banner is love; everything You do and speak is unsearchable love and magnificent glory. Thank you for allowing me entrance into this throne room of grace, dirty and broken and full of complaint. You understood. For this I am eternally grateful. I am Yours.

Your daughter, Robin

TABLE OF CONTENTS

PART TWO

I have written this book for two good reasons. First of all, God Himself has continually pressed me to write since the beginning of this story. At first I thought it as kind of a therapy – conversations between Him and me. And it was good. Then the need to write wore off. God drew me near to Him and we could just converse. But still the unmistakable gentle press of the Holy Spirit to write it *all* down. Because it is not my story – it is His.

Secondly, there are few who have heard it all. I have watched expressions over the years ranging from horror and shock (one girl burst into tears) to the more common response of extraordinary discomfort as I have brought my son's murder into a conversation. More out of consideration for others, I won't bring it up. Different if he had died from cancer or even a car wreck. But murder?

Yet I know human nature and were I not his mother, the individual would be drilling me for details, the more gruesome the better.

This story has that sort of horror, so if you are looking to quench the bizarre appetite we own for the violent, the tragic, and the dark side, you will find it here. But the story is told for a different reason, because as the apostle Paul said; "Yet for our light affliction, there is an exceedingly greater weight of glory." Light affliction? Yes. As the scales have slowly tipped over the last 15 years, my gaze has shifted from the horrendous sight of my son's dead body lying on an ER stretcher to his glorified body, as he rejoices in the presence of a just and loving God; the scale tips and lifts me high into

His glory and grace, to the peculiar joy set before us as we run this race.

This story is dedicated to my son, Spencer, who ran, stumbling, getting up and running again to fall again, and getting up to fall finally and gratefully into the arms of his Lord and Savior, Jesus Christ. Well done.

PART ONE

CHAPTER 1

THE TRAUMA ROOM

Before a tsunami, the tide draws back and recedes way out to sea.

In Thailand on December 26th 2004, curious onlookers and tourists in swimsuits and sunblock ran out onto the exposed sea floor, taking pictures of the fish flopping on the sand. Only a few noticed birds and animals heading the other way, to the high ground, as fast as they could go – because you only have a few minutes of time before that same ocean comes rushing back in, roaring like a jet. It is a black wall of unstoppable fury. It takes every living thing in its way, rolling trucks into stores, tossing bodies like wet towels into trees, its force stronger than 23,000 atomic bombs. Then with the same zeal that the ocean pushed in, it retreats, sucking everything it uprooted back into its belly: homes, cars, babies – the wreckage of a tourist town swirling like crushed shells as the Indian Ocean withdraws back to its place. And the sun shines for the rest of the day, still but for the great wail of loss that pours out across the unfamiliar town.

Midnight already. So far it had been a good night – busy but manageable. It was the height of the flu season, stretchers circled the Emergency Room desk like a wagon train, with IV bags and tubing hanging from poles, bringing life to crumpled bodies under blankets. And it was also Friday night – drunks, fights and falls filled the rooms while the docs stitched away.

I saw a few people I knew. *Cape Cod is a small place,* we say. There's nowhere to run and hide unless you head over the bridge. In the ER you learned a lot of secrets. I saw Mike from church, our eyes met and I half-smiled. He tried to read me – was I safe? He was in the psyche section again, still seeing ghosts from Viet Nam. And I saw Thomas, pacing in Room 11. Must be about 17 now, tall and thin, eyes jumping out from his dark skin, always looks scared. You should be scared left in charge of five younger siblings, I thought, his family always shifting and splitting. He peeked at me from behind the curtain.

"Hey Thomas!" He poked his head out, his smile brief, rocking back and forth on his feet.

"Hey Miss Robin."

Then I saw Jeff and Joe, *Fat Joe* as he was still called after so many years.

"There's Spencer's mom," I heard as I triaged the waiting room, then turned to see Jeff holding a bloody towel to his head. I hadn't seen him in at least four years, but he was still big and husky, with the same childlike smile and shy eyes.

"Still fighting?" I smiled at them both. They were not teens anymore and they looked down, embarrassed.

Later I watched Chris, the ER doc that night, throw some sutures into his scalp while we joked about the old days. I had cared for various wounds during Spencer's worst years, including Fat Joe's broken tooth after it was punched out.

"I'm glad Spencer's fighting days are long gone," I said as Chris left the room. Jeff and Joe nodded and laughed.

"Yeah, that's not Spencer anymore."

Chris looked up from his notes as I came out to the nurses' station.

"You know those guys?"

"Used to," I replied, sitting down. "My son used to hang out with them in high school, and they all fought a lot." I paused. Chris looked back to his chart. He was usually grumpy working nights, and I wasn't sure if he was looking for a conversation.

"I was always scared that Spencer would get stabbed or something. He used to mouth off to anyone," I mused. Chris kept writing. I remembered the black eye, the broken nose, the close calls Spencer told me about much later, when he knew I wouldn't worry.

"Not any more though. He's changed." Chris looked up at me.

"Really? How?" His question startled me, because the answer should be simple. *Because God took that from him. all at once…the anger, the rage. It was a miracle.*

I started to speak, but felt relieved when suddenly Chris was called away to another room. I had left a message for Spence earlier, with no return call. Things seemed better now. But there was something still unsettled that only a mom would pick up on. Spence was never easy, never simple.

Just a few more hours and I am off, I thought as I checked on the drunk in Room 16. An elderly man smiled and waved from beneath a bulky dressing on his head.

"Who's up for a pool?" Kevin, an ER tech, called out across the nurses' station. He thumbed through a small wad of singles in his hand.

"What's the bet?" I asked smiling. I loved Kevin's energy, his boyish smile framed in thick stubble, eyes puffy and dark. At two in the morning you had to try anything to keep the momentum going.

"Your guy in 16," he said. "ETOH level. I guessed 250." A small group was gathering, reaching into pockets for money. Blood alcohol level. This guy's been drinking a long time, I thought.

"417," I said, and Kevin let out a mock gasp.

"Ooooooh… Robin's coming in high! Who else, who else?" Numbers and money were flying as Kevin furiously scribbled. Then I saw Katie walk in. She had trained me in the ER.

"What are you doing here?" I had never seen her on the night shift before.

"I don't know!" she said. "They begged me to come in at three for the day, said we were super busy…" she trailed off, looking at all of the nurses hanging out at the station with doctors and techs, and Kevin counting the money.

"Maybe not!" She laughed, taking off her coat.

"Okay, okay, everyone. The blood work is back on 16," the charge nurse called out. All faces turned her way.

"ETOH 402" she announced. Kevin screened the numbers.

"Robin's got it! I don't believe it!" And he handed a thick stack of ones to me. I pushed it back.

"Coffee and donuts on me!" Cheers erupted, and Kevin took out his pen again. He was the Donut Works go-to-guy; he loved to make the midnight run down the street.

Suddenly the radio crackled and everyone stopped talking and turned towards it, moving closer to hear.

"C-Med to Cape Cod, can you read?"

The charge nurse reached over for the mike. "Cape Cod here, reading you loud and clear."

C-Med only called when it was really bad – bad enough that you would have to pull extra staff, like a Trauma Alert or multiple casualties. Everyone moved closer to listen in.

"We have two stabbings in Yarmouth, both Priority One. ETA 10 minutes, do you read?" Doctors, nurses, techs began to move into position as she pressed down on the mike.

"Yes, C-Med, loud and clear. Cape Cod out."

"Katie, you and Susan take Trauma Nurse left and right," Chris ordered. I looked at Katie. I was fairly new to the ER, so the more experienced nurses took the hardest cases, but it was a good way to learn, to watch.

"Can Robin be the scribe?" she asked. Chris shrugged and nodded. I was in, and we all moved towards Room 2, the Trauma Room.

The young man with the dark blue eyes didn't want to be there, and he had told his girlfriend, Arheesia, that he would not be coming around anymore that same night. But he stayed, feeling that it could be dangerous for her if he left, and maybe others. He was no stranger to fighting, to the machismo drive behind retaliation, and although he didn't even understand the issue, he knew there was a fight going on somewhere. So he retreated to an upstairs bedroom, tired. He had also told Arheesia he wasn't feeling well, but there was more to it than that. From the bed, he looked up to the sky, the stars so clear. *God, are you there?*

He told his friend Jermaine not to go back, to let it go, but Jermaine hadn't changed in that way, still bullheaded, still a fighter. He was not, he *had* changed and maybe that's why he told Arheesia he wouldn't be coming around anymore. He didn't belong. Tired, he lay down, wondering where on earth he did belong.

He had just drifted off, when he heard the crash, no, more like felt the crash. The whole house moved, the front door blasted right off the hinges and then there were screams. He jumped out of bed, wearing only jeans and a t-shirt, and ran towards the noise, taking the staircase in three strides. He knew what it was and he stepped right into it, into the rage, not to fight, but to rescue, to save.

The girl behind the donut counter stacked the coffees into the box, and waited patiently for Kevin to pick the last donut. It was three in the morning and Kevin was the best thing she'd seen all night on the graveyard shift. She liked to flirt just a little with him, although she knew he was married, but he was also a gentleman so it was fun and that was all. Kevin made everyone smile.

"And one Boston Crème."

She bagged the donuts and set them on the counter next to the coffees while he thumbed through the wad of singles.

Sirens drew closer, and Kevin squinted through the plate glass.

"Yarmouth," he read on the side of the truck, as it veered around the corner. He paid her, leaving a big tip and grabbed the bag.

"It's never good at three in the morning." He nodded to the young girl behind the counter, the smile gone, as he strode quickly out the door.

"Trauma alert: ETA 10 minutes" sounded on the overhead. I followed Katie into Room 2, the Trauma Room. It was the pride of the new ER, equipped with just about any piece of equipment you could need.

The nurses and techs were donning protective gowns when the charge nurse looked in and said Yarmouth had called. One of the Priority Ones' had been upgraded to a Code Blue; no vital signs. Scott, one of the techs, began to peel off his gown saying, "We probably won't be needing this then," and the two nurses chuckled and pulled their gowns off too. When you're new like me, you are silent a lot because by the time your brain understands what's going on in an ER, everyone's moved on to the next thing. *No pulse, no blood flow – no mess. Okay, I get it.*

"They're here!" the unit clerk yelled from the hall and I heard the diesel sound of the ambulance rumbling outside of the door. The hall was crowded with hospital staff from every unit, and the conversation was light and edgy. As the doors slid open, a rush of frigid January air mixed with exhaust filled the hall, then an EMT holding up an IV bag, pushing a stretcher fast, another medic doing chest compressions, and another squeezing an Ambu bag, giving breath to the lifeless body. I turned back into the Trauma Room.

I reach for my glasses, realizing everything is blurry, but I can see a stretcher and a very pale body push quickly past me to the middle of the room, where the body is shifted onto our gurney. The paramedic holds up his report, rolled into a tube and looks at me, like he wants to give it to someone.

"Do we have a name?" I ask. The room is bustling, full of noise and people suddenly. A medic will normally give a short report, at least a name, but he just holds it up, like a baton and stares at me. Then he turns abruptly and leaves, taking the report still clenched in his hand.

Chris comes in and moves to the stretcher, starting at the head working down. Katie and Sue are on the left and right, checking his lines, fluid, airway and other equipment, but then Sue is called away when the Priority One arrives. Katie watches Chris and waits for orders. My job, as scribe, is to write down everything I hear and see.

The trauma flow sheet is three pages across and takes up the whole bedside table I have in front of me as I stand out of the way, against the wall. I am a Trauma Certified Nurse, I took the class, so I know how it's supposed to run; head to toe, then turn the body over, view the back. I put on my glasses and I scan the sheet. There's a drawing of a body, front and back and my job is to fill it in, every bruise, scratch and mark.

The techs pull out their trauma scissors and work at cutting off the jeans, revealing a large stab wound to the left thigh.

"Head's okay," Chris calls out, then lifts the lids. "Pupils fixed and dilated," he says, quieter now.

A respiratory therapist wheels in a ventilator, while another continues to pump the purple Ambu bag. Two IV bags hang above the body, clamps off or "wide open," running into both arms. I look up to the monitor over the stretcher. No blood pressure. Just to be sure, I walk over to the body and make sure the cuff is on right, smoothing the fabric over the right arm. The screen shows a rhythm, short spikes running across the screen, and if you didn't know any better you'd say it was good, but it wasn't. Pulseless Electrical Activity, or PEA was the name of this rhythm. *DEAD* someone would spell beneath their breath in class, causing a light ripple of laughter across the room.

"Two stab wounds to the chest; top right and left center," Chris continued his exam. He lifted a large bulky dressing over the left chest. There was a small stain, but no blood from the large two-inch gash. Chris shook his head and stepped back, reflecting a moment. He turned to Scott, who was looking over his shoulder. "Go get the rib spreaders," and Scott wheeled around and quickly left the room.

There was still a lot of motion, and once more I stepped out from behind my table in the corner, then forgot why. I felt suddenly confused and unfocused, and a nurse who was moving between the trauma room and Room 5, where the other stabbing victim was being worked on, grabbed me by the shoulders and moved me out of the way.

I went back behind the table, to concentrate again on documenting, carefully marking the stab wounds as small dashes on the paper body and tracking the vital signs every five minutes, but there were none, and as each minute went

by, everyone in the trauma room was coming to the same con-
clusion. A sigh, shaking the head, staring at the monitor, the
IV fluid infusing into a bloodless body.

Scott showed up with a sterile package, dropped it on
the table next to Chris and started to unwrap it. Chris took
a scalpel and made a long incision below the stab wound. It
was a last chance, and a desperate one but there was nothing
at all to lose. Scott pulled out the spreaders and handed them
to Chris, as he hitched them on either side of his incision, rib
to rib, then squeezed. The arms of the instrument lifted and
spread the ribs apart.

"Hold this right here," he said, and Scott grabbed the
spreader and held it, exposing the heart. Scott was an Air
Force corpsman and he was confident in the traumas.

Chris reached into the opening and gently wrapped his
hand around the lower half of the heart, the ventricles, the
main part of the pump. And there, for all to see, was a huge
gash going right through the left ventricle. The young heart
had diligently pumped all of this man's blood through the hole
until there was no more to pump. Then it stopped, still sending false signals through the empty chambers. Chris looked at
me, looked at Katie and Scott and simply said, "Let's call it."
And at 0339, next to the small box that said *Expired,* I made a
check and wrote the time.

We move slower now in the trauma room, although there
is still a lot of activity in Room 5, and now cops are arriving,
some in uniforms, some in plain clothes. I remember how my
mother always said, "There's a mother somewhere who will
never be the same" every time a child died, and I think of
that now, as Patrick, the patient liaison comes into the room,
looking for an ID.

"Watch out!" Katie says suddenly, pushing me back as I hear the sound of something spilling onto the floor. It's blood, likely the only blood still left in this guy's body after Chris cut open his chest. It hits the floor and splashes onto my shoes. ER nursing is like that, and we joke about leaving our shoes outside. Now this.

Patrick and Katie are thumbing through the wallet as I wipe off my shoes, then I look over their shoulder. Suddenly my eyes focus on a name: *Spencer Macleod.* It's on a bank-card, my son's bank, Cape Cod Trust, with the picture of seagulls and sand dunes. My mind jumps up, like being slapped awake.

"What's this guy doing with my son's bank card?" I say.

Katie and Patrick don't move, then Katie asks, "Are you sure it's your son's?" which is an irritating question to me, and I am aware I am angry. Then more. *Spencer Macleod* on a gym membership card. I feel something rushing through my body, hot, like liquid fire.

"What's this guy doing with my son's wallet?" My voice sounds strange, distant; my legs feel different.

Look at the body. I realize I have to turn around, I have to walk to the stretcher and my legs begin to move.

I had not looked at the face, simply because there was no injury to the face. I turn to the stretcher and walk. In my memory, everything is dark, not black dark; sort of sepia, dim, and my legs are pushing, like I'm in deep water, in an under-tow. One, two, three steps.

I don't even reach the face. There on the right arm, where the blood pressure cuff had been, was a small plain tattoo, engraved with a needle and a Bic pen, a tattoo we laughed about, but I was mad when I first saw it seven years ago. His friend Jermaine had given Spence that tattoo when they were teens, and there was none like it.

"That's my son," I said, maybe more than once, as I turned away, my legs quitting. It was getting darker. I felt arms from everywhere but I saw nothing. People said I screamed, an unnatural sound they would not forget, but in my mind the sound was gone too.

"I can't, I can't," I said over and over. I was talking to God. Nobody knew I was talking to God. But I had to tell him; He had it wrong, not this. *I can't.* Arms brought me into Room 3.

I'm in a chair, in the corner of the small exam room, and Spencer's wallet is in my hands. I look through it, noting he must've misplaced his license again. I find a card that says this:

For I know the thoughts that I think toward you, says the Lord, thoughts of peace and not of evil, to give you a future and a hope. Jeremiah 29:11

Hope? I lifted my face upwards, but before I could even ask the next thing, just one thing, I heard a voice like thunder roll down from way up high like an avalanche into a place in my soul I never knew was there.

I AM GOD. DON'T ASK WHY.

And I was silenced, like a shushed child; I sat in my corner chair, looking down at the wallet I held in my hands.

Peter, Spencer's dad, came into the room, and as soon as I saw his face I knew no one had told him. I jumped up and my eyes told him before my words.

"He died. Spencer's dead," I blurted out. I watched the words smash him, take him down. Peter slowly shook his head.

"Someone killed him." My voice sounded high, unnatural. I felt I had to explain all this.

"No!" He grabbed a chair and threw it to the floor, then fell to his knees beside it. *No, no, no.* A security guard rushed in but stopped, saw Peter hunched over sobbing and me sitting beside him, my hand on his back.

"I'm sorry, Pete. I'm so sorry." I feel dead and dull like driftwood, but I am here, this is real.

Cops come in, questions without answers. A detective with a notepad tries not to look at me.

Why was Spencer there?

Who was in the house?

He asks about a girl, a child upstairs. Names. I shake my head, I know nothing, and so he puts his pen away and leaves. Then a tall officer with soft eyes meets me in the hall, bends to my face and says, "Your son saved someone's life. We will have arrests made by the end of the day." He stood up straight, nodded and turned away. A paramedic cried into her hands at the desk while another one held her.

I asked one of the nurses to get Spencer ready for his dad to see. He returned after a short time and motioned us in. My husband, C.B., had arrived with my youngest son Jake, who sat with Kevin at the nurses' station playing video games. C.B., Peter and I walked into the Trauma Room together.

I had seen Spence, but I hadn't seen his face. But now as we walked into the trauma room, surrounded by steel and chrome and lifeless machines with silent monitors, now as we reached the stretcher with the sheet draped up to the chest, we stopped all at once, and stared at the face of the young man, with eyes like the ocean that were closed forever.

"He looks beautiful," Peter spoke just above a whisper.

"He really does," C.B. said. "He's...glowing."

I studied his face. There was a tangible...glow? Dead people don't glow. I had seen many of them in all my years of nursing. In fact, I never got used to the ghastly pallor of a lifeless face, the corpse taking over, the last expression of surprise. But Spence looked...peaceful, and also somewhat determined and serious, like he had completed a mission. I remembered the expression he was born with, almost 22 years ago and three flights upstairs; the little face so certain, like he knew what he was here for. I touched his hair, running my fingers through it like so many times before. It was thick and oily.

"His hand is cold," Peter said, his voice breaking. He had reached under the sheet to touch him.

I moved towards the door, suddenly wanting to go.

Katie helped me get my things. I looked at the photo on my locker. Three sons, sitting together on a swinging bench under a live oak tree, taken last summer on Edisto Island, our favorite place. Three sons and me always behind the camera. Miles, the middle one, with his arms folded, confident after his freshman year in college. Jake, the little brother is on Miles' right, with a wide smile, ten years behind Miles, twelve behind Spence, the little-man, and Spence, to Miles' right. He is sitting back a bit, the shy smile looking at me through the camera. We are all together and there is love in each face. I take my stuff from the locker, and shutting the door, leave the picture behind.

Outside the air grabbed at my breath as I walked to the car, sleepy Jake stumbling behind me along with a security guard. Lights and colors flashed from a gridlock of parked cars; state troopers, cops from three different towns. *That's right, there has been a murder.*

The security guard asked again if I was okay to drive. *Yes,* I told him grabbing Jake to come with me. After I took off down the road, I realized I wasn't okay, but kept going anyway, turning onto Route 28 into Yarmouth, retracing the route an ambulance had taken just two hours earlier with a young man in the back, his body like alabaster, without blood.

The sun was edging up on a clear sky, but Cape Cod was still asleep. I drove slowly, past the darkened seafood restaurants, the frozen mini golf courses, the streetlights pulling the car forward, a nine-year-old boy silent beside me. In the dark I was unsure if he was asleep or just quiet.

I thought of Miles, his brother, 600 miles away in Maryland, asleep, maybe dreaming normal dreams that college kids dream; basketball, girls, geology exams, flying dreams. It seemed so unfair to break the dreams, to wake him up like this: *Your brother is dead, Miles. Murdered.* Or maybe say "killed," it sounds better than *murdered.*

Across from our street, the Cumberland Farms minimart was ablaze with mostly construction workers on their way to work, pocketing cigarettes and hot coffee, trucks warming up outside. *This is just another day,* I thought. It's just a day, and I noticed the sky had turned from navy blue to cobalt. No clouds. A clear January day.

I put on the blinker and steered the car onto my empty road, slowly, carefully. Jake was awake and silent, looking straight ahead. Did he notice? Our street, the darkened houses and the little gray-shingled house on the corner under the tall pine tree, our house, everything, was somehow different, but I couldn't pick out why. I squinted into the dawn light. Fake, it all looked pretend, like it would fall over with just one breath.

The bleached clamshells in the driveway crunched under the tires as I came to a slow stop. I waited before getting out, looking again to the strange house, the fence covered in rosa rugosa, the ivy searching the chimney for warmth.

"C'mon, Jakey. Let's go in." He stayed still, maybe uncertain too. I opened my door and stepped out.

CHAPTER 2

THE MAPLE TREE

In my memory I can smell the tree before I see it. Winter, the earthiness of cold bark; spring, the tease of new life, fragile leaves uncurling like babies' hands, the grass beneath waking up; summer, the fullness of green cover, sharing the heavy damp air, the rain on the hot tar below, cooling down the cement street, the steam rising. Then fall, sweet smell of decay, of smoke and the leaves turning into fire, and fire falling, and it was all play.

The maple tree was in the front yard of the old English Tudor home, my home, bending way over the busy street, which started a mile north at a bridge over the train tracks. Hendrie Avenue wound past Riverside Elementary School, a playground, a stone wall where teenagers smoked and flirted, a Junior High school, then down the hill past my house and the maple tree, abruptly ending across from Ada's.

Ada's was a candy store to kids, a place to grab a paper for most commuters walking to the train station nearby, and a quick stop for cigarettes and soda. It was said that Ada made the best bologna sandwich in town, just mayo on Wonder bread, but I never ate one. Teens hung out in the back room, sitting on soda coolers, thumbing through Archie comics, or on the big cement porch, where they could be loud. The small dirty-white house encased in a chain link fence betrayed the comfortable upper-middle class of Riverside.

Ada opened that store years before zoning by-laws existed, with her two sisters, Rita and Cheta, who lived in Cos Cob, "on the other side of the Post Road," my mother would explain, because they were "I-talians." And there she stayed, scooping penny candy into little brown bags long after it was worth just a penny, with a long bony finger on the pulse of a well-to-do community, watching the drugs of the 60's sweep away many children, divorce split many pretty homes and death tap someone close by on the shoulder. People were just people to Ada.

She tried to help me when I started getting in trouble with the law. She'd throw the teens out of the back and clear off the cooler for my schoolbooks, pulling up a chair for me at my makeshift desk.

"Do your homework, Birdie," she'd say, grinding a pencil to a sharp point in an oily pencil sharpener that hung next to the Twinkie rack. Ada knew that behind the doors of the pretty Tudor home up the street there was chaos, but she didn't try to figure it out or counsel me. And she didn't try to help for love or valor either; she just did what she could with what she had.

"Ya never know!" she would say, smoke releasing through her teeth as she shook her head. Then she'd set her Pall Mall in the big glass ashtray next to the cash register and take your money.

The maple tree that faced my house had a long branch that bent towards the ground, inviting a climb. Or now I wonder if I bent it down from jumping on it so much, grabbing the limb, swinging my legs up over the top and shimmying up to the trunk. From there it was an easy climb to my seat – a perfect fork jutting out over the street from the trunk, tucked up into the cover of the branches, tucked out of sight, but close enough to hear and see everything.

The summer of 1964 was a respite of relief. The previous school year, half second grade and half third, was confusing. I don't know why I couldn't be still or quiet. There in the class-room, with so much time going by, second hand by second hand, the desks became a jungle gym and my gorilla imitation made everyone laugh.

Miss Troutwein, my second grade teacher, was not amused, and had used my long ponytail as a leash more than once, dragging me across the floor. The worst part was seeing the other kids' faces. Nervous, scared. Other teachers didn't do this. Then the time she slapped me hard on the cheek, bending her face down to mine so she could whisper, "I'm in control here!"

I never would tell my parents that I was so bad she had to do that.

On a good day I would get sent to Mr. Simpkin's office, the principal, who was not scary at all; in fact, I think he liked my company. He would put me to work, moving stacks of paper around his roomy office, calling me his "helper." He looked small behind the massive mahogany desk. Often he would smoke his pipe and the smoke smelled like fall leaves burning, and circled his thick white hair and shaggy eyebrows that arched over his glasses.

Sometimes I would catch him looking out of the tall windows, over the entrance to the school, the parade of sta-tion wagons spilling children onto the sidewalk. But he was looking beyond, into the towering pines and oaks, past the stacks of paper and the drone of the school day.

At the end of the day, he would move over to the xylophone next to a microphone on a short stand, and he would ceremoniously hand me the long stick with the soft pad at the end. He had taught me the three-toned ring when I was in first grade, exiled from Mrs. Wilson's class. It signaled the end of the day and announcements, and as I held the stick poised over the small keys, I waited for his nod. After the three strokes, he always smiled at me, and that smile was the best part of my whole six years at Riverside Elementary School. He leaned into the microphone.

"Good afternoon, ladies and gentlemen. This is Mr. Simpkins…" Secretly, I thought he was just like me, that he couldn't wait to leave and go play.

"The school wants you to skip a grade," my mother said one day, like you would say, *The dentist wants to drill your teeth.* She looked tired, and men with briefcases filled with puzzles and pictures had told her what she wanted to hear. I was smart enough. The plan was to have me skip a grade by moving into third grade in January, completing two whole grades in half the time. The goal was to keep me so busy I would not have time to disrupt the class. It didn't work.

I thought of all these things, in bits and pieces, over the summer between the maple leaves, sticking the pods to my nose and letting inchworms crawl up my arm. I'd see Miss Troutwein and her eyes that didn't match her smile, then Mr. Simpkins looking at me over his wire-rim glasses, his jowls gently shaking as he shook his head. Then Miss Krumich, the third grade teacher, who seemed nice at first. She never came close to me like Miss Troutwein. But sometimes that was worse because everyone could hear her when she said, "Now Robin, you don't want me to send you back to second grade, do you?" But it wasn't a real question because she just smiled and went on to the next thing. I could feel my face turn hot, like I might cry, and all of the kids would laugh and point at me without making noise.

My brother Timmy was in the third grade with me, which was a big plus, because everyone liked Timmy. He was a diplomat, always settling arguments and making people laugh. I think he was the only third grader who liked me, and the next year we could be in the same class, according to Mr. Simpkins.

At the beach, which was just a short drive from our house, my mom would spread a blanket where she'd sit with her big straw hat on next to my baby sister, Caroline who also had a big hat on, and watch me swim with my brothers: Bob, four years older, Tim just a year older and Graham, who was only four then and stayed in the shallow water. When our lips were blue, she'd call us out and Timmy and I would flop down belly-first on the hot sand, letting the sun dry our backs, and we'd discuss fourth grade, which I was more troubled over than Tim.

"I hope we get Miss Eagen," he'd say, sifting the sand through his fingers. "I hear she's nice." And I would just say *Yeah,* because Timmy knew inside stuff like that. He never had a bad teacher like Miss Troutwein, but he never got everyone mad either.

July meant summer day camp; the boys were bussed off to a camp on an island and the girls were shuttled down to the beach. We made potholders, then lay down on our stomachs in the shallow water and kicked our legs. This was learning how to swim, they said.

When I got home, Timmy was there, telling me about an island and swimming out deep to a float where you could jump in over your head and using knives to carve soap and make totem poles. I listened wistfully to tales of another world that girls were banned from, thriving on his stories of island adventure.

Then one day, Timmy was not there. Mrs. Graham, our neighbor was in the kitchen, and she gave me a funny look when I came home, like she didn't know who I was even though I played with her daughter Margaret when there was no one else to play with.

"Timmy fainted," she said. "Your parents are at the hospital." Then she went back to cooking.

Parents? Why would my dad be there? He was in New York City every day, doing Public Relations, he called it.

I sat on the cold radiator in the dining room and looked out of the large bay window, pushing the white sheer curtains aside. Timmy fainted twice before, once at the neighbor's, and once playing soccer. That time they carried him to the side of the field where I stood holding up my bike. When he opened his eyes, he looked right at me. He wasn't scared. He was so brave.

I bounced the heel of my sneaker off of the cool cast iron. The curtains smelled like my dad's shirts. *Maybe Timmy is dead*, I thought. I had only had pets die, like my canary after I took her outside so she could see some real trees. And I saw cowboys die on TV. Something was not right anyway.

Then I saw what I was waiting for – the Ford station wagon pulling into the driveway. My father was driving, still in his suit and tie, with my mother next to him. They got out of the car so slow it seemed, and Timmy was not with them. Mrs. Graham went out to meet them, and I could see them walk around the house, talking and looking down at the bushes and flowers, then she turned and walked home.

Bob, my oldest brother, came downstairs as my parents came inside and we all sat in the living room – mom and dad on one side and Bob and me on the other.

"Timmy's dead," my dad said, just like that, and he watched us to see what was next. Mom stared at the carpet. Bob didn't move, but I started crying and ran to my father's arms. My mom said, "Bobby?" and Bob went to my mom and he cried too. Then we were told to go outside and play. I kept crying when I was in the back yard and Dad yelled at me from the kitchen window to knock it off.

Next door, my friends Ricky and Bucky were up in their apple tree and I clambered up beside them. They already knew Timmy was dead and their mom was on the porch sobbing, which seemed funny to me because my mom didn't cry at all.

Instead of dinnertime, there were lots of people with casseroles in their hands and crumpled up tissues. It was grown-up stuff and we had all been trained to stay away when grown-ups were around, so I went out to the maple tree and shimmied up to my place in the branches, where I could watch people walk by carrying more food, talking, or driving by slow. The front door opened and I saw Graham, my little brother step out. He couldn't see me in the tree.

"Hey Boo!" I called.

"Birdie, where are you?" He looked scared so I climbed down the tree, dropping to the ground from the last branch, and sat next to him on the front steps, our dirty knees touching. We were quiet together, and the sky was slowly giving way to the night.

"Stars!" Graham's little finger thrust upward towards the darkest part of the sky. I wondered if he knew Timmy was dead. Mom said Timmy was with God now.

"Timmy's up there," I said, lining my finger up with his, towards the eastern sky.

His little hand came down and rested on my arm, but we both still looked up, into the overtaking darkness.

"Where?" Graham asked, finally.

Where? It seemed to echo inside of me. I scanned the sky, the stars, the rising moon. Where is God, anyway?

In 1969, the first man walked on the moon. Richard Nixon took office and Charlie Manson made headlines. The Beatles had their last concert together and the draft lottery for Viet Nam was churning out numbers. Half a million people showed up at a farm in Woodstock, upstate New York for a big concert. Peace. Freedom. Revolution. We were killing and making love. *Easy Rider* was released and *Sesame Street* aired.

My mom called me out to the back porch and said, "Your dad lost his job."

My dad tucked me in a few weeks later and said, "I'm leaving your mom."

I did not climb the maple tree anymore.

Instead I ran away.

CHAPTER 3

RUNNING

"Freedom's just another word for nothin' left to lose"

– JANIS JOPLIN

I became good at running away. The summer of '69, my dad arranged for me to go off to an Arabian horse breeding ranch in Kansas, which his friend Jim owned. The conversation went something like this:

> Bob (my dad): My daughter is driving us crazy. Keeps running away. (Pause)
>
> Jim: Send her out to us, Bob. There's nowhere to run in Kansas!
>
> Bob: That's a great idea! Hey, let me buy you another drink!
>
> Jim: Another great idea (laughs). Let's toast to it!

I landed in Kansas City, age 13, wearing white socks and a mini skirt. I had put Coppertone tanner on my legs, and when Jim and his family failed to meet me as I stepped off the plane onto the tarmac, I began to sweat in the Missouri heat, making little orange rivers run into my socks. Finally they showed up: Jim, his scared wife and their depressed daughter, Julie, a couple years younger than me.

I remember I loved the Kansas sky, how it drew my attention away from the dry cracked land. I loved riding through dusty cornfields bareback, not knowing where it would end. At night we would sit out on the front porch and stare into the wide horizon as the sky grew dark and swept away the heat.

It turns out Jim and his wife were not faring any better than my parents. There were whispers of divorce, even a suicide attempt. Little Julie and I didn't talk much – she always looked like she would cry, so we got used to our painful silence and letting our confusion stay unanswered.

At night the sky exploded with stars, and it occurred to me that we – Julie, her parents and I, were small and full of problems. Small people with big problems and no answers.

I returned home early, in time to run away for the rest of the summer before school started.

1970

Hippies don't vacuum.

I didn't say it, but I thought it immediately when Ed, the lead hippie of the commune, handed me the upright.

I had hitched all the way to Old Saybrook, envisioning Arlo Guthrie and a teepee, hash brownies in the wood burning stove and a lot of wine. Instead I found a carpeted duplex in a crowded suburb. Ed was as wary of me as I was of him. I was 14. I looked older than that, but I lacked the aura of sophistication that the older hippies had.

However, I could shoplift, and raised some eyebrows when I returned home with sneakers in my overalls. Soon I was taking orders and everyone forgot about vacuuming. The overalls could accommodate shoes, clothing, wine bottles and cigarette cartons. I had no fear, certainly no remorse.

I was gaining respect in my new position when I was nabbed leaving a Grant's department store one night. The manager was not unkind or unreasonable when he called the police and handed me over to the authorities. In fact he looked sad about it, and I wanted to tell him it was the right thing to do.

After giving the cops the wrong name for two hours, I finally broke and they reached my dad. He never looked drunk when he was drunk – he became hyper and got this peculiar smile that people loved and thought he was a great guy. But it scared me.

It was a long ride home, the Volkswagen bus hopping all over the Connecticut turnpike. He was mad, but smiling.

"You really know how to blow it big, Rob." He shook his head. Silence.

"Your mother's just about done in." He veered into the next lane. Traffic was light so I wasn't too scared. "You really messed up big, kiddo. How does reform school sound? "

He threatened me often with reform school, describing gray jumpsuits and bars and various means of torture, which now I think he borrowed from Japanese WWII camps. He lit another cigarette, the car jumping down the highway.

I could see the smile in the flash of the match.

"You really did it now."

CHAPTER 4

BEDLAM

Where does one go from a world of insanity?
Somewhere on the other side of despair.

– T. S. ELIOT

August 1977

At dusk, the lights flickered on in the summer heat across New York City. From ten stories up I could see past Harlem, to the charcoal shadow of Wards Island, across the Harlem River. How appropriate, I thought, that Harlem was darker than the other view from the psychiatric ward at Mount Sinai Hospital, looking downtown to the tony Upper East Side. But I preferred this window, the window seat below it, where I could curl up and watch the day fade into the thick city air. It felt safe up high.

It was 1977, the summer Elvis died and Son of Sam was finally caught; it was my third New York City summer since sliding anonymously into the sweltering streets of Manhattan at age 19, during a garbage strike and heat wave. After the trash reached second story windows and the thermometer reached 100, the mayor listened.

I loved it at first. I felt big and heady with possibilities – I could switch lives like playing dress-up, starting out as a waitress in a cocktail lounge in the theatre district. There I met Tony and Paulie, who were much older than me, two bottom–rung bookies from Brooklyn. Tony drove a pale yellow Cadillac convertible and tended bar. He taught me how to smoke cigars and drink Johnnie Walker Red, how to spot a scam or a pimp. We would go to Vinnie's, an old midtown Mafia lounge and I'd watch Paulie's big droopy eyes mist over when the piano player sang the Frank Sinatra medley.

Then I moved to the Lower East Side to a loft with my brother Bob. I decided I was a poet, and Bob was a musician so we both drank a lot, sometimes perched on the roof ledge of our four-story walk-up with a six-pack or two of beer between us. The traffic from First Avenue rumbled below, loosening the mortar between the bricks of the old building, thick exhaust rising past us into the greasy night. We would talk and laugh loud like you can with family, rocking back and forth above the streetlights, a little more with each beer – songs and dreams rising like campfire smoke into the haze above.

I fell in love often, then got bored quickly, leaving a trail of carnage behind me. After a few years, I moved to another loft with a bass player and his recording studio on lower Broadway, where it was quiet and desolate except for a soup kitchen and a few bodegas. We were on the fifth floor but you could hear the homeless men bumming change below. The lights would turn uptown and a low rumble of taxis and tourists would surge past heading to China Town and Wall St., leaving a cavernous echo between the tall empty buildings around us. I would sit out on the fire escape, as if I was waiting to be rescued.

One night the bass player told me he didn't love me anymore, he was tired of trying to love a drunk and wanted to love someone else, someone who laughed and smiled a lot. He was becoming successful too, playing uptown on the real Broadway. So I left.

My father lived in mid-town Manhattan and my brother was still on the Lower East Side, but I didn't want to tell them that I was all alone. I didn't want anyone to know I had lost everything, which wasn't much, and I didn't even see it coming. I was running out of lives to change into.

I rented the first place I could find; a narrow fifth floor walkup in Gramercy. Summer had begun and the smell of curry and decaying trash drifted up the common alleyway my windows opened out onto. At night, the fighting began. Sometimes I could detect three or four different languages; the English was the worst to listen to. And the heat. I would sweat lying still as a stone, the air carrying exhaust, grease, trash and rage into my window, covering all of me. I thought about death.

The lithium wasn't working.

Once a month I traveled uptown to the Lithium clinic to get my blood drawn. My mother and grandfather had set me up at Mt. Sinai Hospital with high hopes for this new drug. They said I was just like Grandma, who died slowly, like a houseplant you forgot to water. *Manic-depressive*, they whispered over her grave. Lithium was supposed to change all that. It was supposed to change me.

There, at the clinic, I met with Dr. Lieberman, a shy psychiatrist with flushed cheeks wearing a Yarmulke. I talked, he looked into his lap at a notepad, scribbling. When he looked up, it was my signal to go.

But this one day, after I talked, he picked up the phone and mumbled a few words, then hung up. Within ten seconds a security guard opened the door and gently explained to me that I could not leave. I was tired and let him lead me like a lost child to the tenth floor, a safe place for now, he said. Committed. I was 21.

I don't think there are many truly crazy people in the world. A part of me wanted to swan dive into madness, to go deep until it became a part of me, like breathing. But like most people at Mount Sinai Hospital, I was not crazy, just broken.

Mary Ellen kept a small American Tourister suitcase packed at all times. She said if you need a place to stay, tell them you want to kill yourself or someone else. "They'll let you right in!" Her suitcase was pink and she always wore dresses, reminding me of Dorothy in the Wizard of Oz.

"This place is nice," she said with some expertise, scanning the art room, then frowned. "But stay away from Bellevue."

Sue, on the other hand, was crazy. She would jump on her bed, naked, for hours, drawing a small mixed crowd. It was entertaining for a brief time, but eventually it just added to your despair. And I remember a little Hispanic man who would slam his head on the floor, sobbing, tears mixing with blood, until he was lifted away, and the medication would hush the pain and bring silence. Sometimes I wondered what made him so broken, what kind of memory would want to make you split your head open just to get it out.

After dinner, visitors would come and my brother Bob would round the corner, sweaty and frazzled after driving a truck from one end of Manhattan to the other through mid-town rush hour in August. Most of the time I couldn't talk, but he was there every single day. He would sit beside me, requiring nothing, but the silence between us was comforting somehow. After a while he'd smile and squeeze my hand, then disappear through locked doors.

Then I would move to the small bench under the large window overlooking Harlem. As the sky above darkened, I could see lights turn on, blinking through the heat. Other buildings remained dark, but I could see shades in the windows, a plant behind bars. Maybe life.

The sky was dark now, and I wondered if the people in Harlem wanted to die too, if there was someone like me, looking up into the sky and saying, "What happened?"

From the other end of the hall I could hear big Helen humming, the night nurse, making her way towards me, her large frame never in a hurry.

"She's in her favorite place," she chided. Her arms came over and around me, smelling of lotion and a hint of body odor. It was Helen smell and it was better than Valium.

"Whatchu doing child?" I turned and looked away. I wanted to cry but it was not in me. "The Lord sure loves you girl."

Love. This is love?

"Let's go, sweetheart," she gently pulled me from the seat. "Another day done. I'll tuck you in."

A soft chuckle rolled off her. And she did tuck me in, clean white sheets and five medications. Another day was done.

CHAPTER 5

THE OUTERMOST

You can't run away from trouble.
There ain't no place that far.

– UNCLE REMUS

1979

Cape Cod stretched out gray and wet beyond the van windows. I never saw so many ugly little pine trees, "scrub pines" they were called, dwarfed and twisted by a constant northeast wind whipping salt and ice across the desolate landscape. I had heard of this place off and on over the years, but never came this way. Vacations either took my family north to Maine, where my father's family lived, or south, to Edisto Island off the coast of South Carolina; my mother's corner.

I had told my boyfriend, Peter MacLeod, that I was leaving, so the Cape was his idea. I had returned briefly to New Jersey, where he lived, after leaving New York City, restless and mapping out my next move. My original intent was Edisto, but I wasn't sure where I would fit in. I had spent the summer before there, landing on my cousins' cattle ranch on a jet stream of Jack Daniels and cocaine. I told them I would work for my stay.

They didn't know much about me, that I was afraid of psyche wards and the electric violence of a city heat wave, of men and falling in love. At an age when most girls were finishing college, I was the free-range poet from New York City. But they took me in, and there, in the simple rhythm of this hidden coastal island, I learned how to bale hay, cast a shrimp net and can bushels of tomatoes.

J.G was my grandfather's first cousin. They grew up side by side on the coastal inlets of Edisto Island. My grandpa left after medical school for good, but J.G. stayed put and managed to hold on to the 400 acre tract through farming, cattle ranching and a lot of sweat and prayer. He and Marian were in their sixties then; J.G. was sunbaked bone and sinew, eyes pale blue and mostly silent, his speech a mix of Carolina coast and Gullah. Marian was a teacher from the mountains who loved this man with an amused sideways glance and could out-work, walk and swim me on any day. He called her "girly".

They were the first real Christians I ever met, and they showed me something else I never knew – grace. In the Carolina heat, in a broken down truck, across a freshly plowed field of dirt and dung, on the worn steps of a church, I grasped the patient hand of God, and learned a few things. I stayed sober that summer, inhaling the salt marsh air and exhaling my fear. I didn't want to leave but somehow I knew it was more than a beautiful island – it was a time, a meeting place. I returned to New York knowing I was not the same.

Eight hundred miles north on the same coast, Cape Cod jutted out into the ocean like a defiant arm, calling men home from sea, beckoning those on land to keep running until you had to stop at the water's edge. The sky, the ocean, the towns we drove through, were a mixed palette of gray and beige. It was March, it was not lovely, but the wild beauty, different than Edisto, drew me. This was harsh and uninviting, whereas Edisto begged you to slow down and stay a while.

Sleet blew sideways, frosting everything exposed to the North Atlantic. The few humans that could make it through a Cape winter in the 70's huddled in isolation that inspired visions, poetry and drinking a lot. I peered out of the old van windows, as Peter and a few friends passed a bottle of Mateus around. It was a good fit.

A month later, I packed up my Volkswagen bus with everything I owned; a steamer trunk my mother had given me, some peacock feathers, a sleeping bag and a pound of pot. The weed was obtained on good faith from a friend of a friend in the city. I had only one hundred dollars to my name, so the pot was intended to boost my finances once I settled.

I left New Jersey in the morning and drove to Cape Cod, weaving through the small towns until the sun started to go down and I realized that Cape Cod is much colder than the mainland in April. Pulling into Wellfleet, I noticed a small market at the top of Main Street. As I paid for two bananas, I asked the cashier if she knew of anywhere to stay. She looked at me for a moment, then handed me a key from her key chain.

"It's small, with only a wood stove but you can have it for a little while if you want it. My husband will bring over some wood."

I had landed.

Peter came up in May with the spring. Peeper frogs called up from the marsh at sunset and the wind turned around and came up from the south, carrying Rosa Rugosa blooms and scallop shells drying in the sun. The fishermen rubbed their eyes and dropped down their clamming rakes, the carpenter's hammer clawed at splintered shingles.

I was not a good drug dealer. We smoked some of the pound, sold some and gave away the rest, and the profit made some guy I never knew in New York City mad at me. Summer arrived with ten thousand people mostly from New Jersey and Ohio and I served drinks to them in a bar tucked into a dune overlooking the ocean. Then I started to feel sick. I couldn't even drink.

"Rob, I think you're pregnant," Peter said.

Our parents were skeptical but resigned.

We got married in a Catholic chapel by a priest who was an intellectual friend of my mother's. He asked about our denominational affiliation.

Presbyterian, I said. I thought of Reverend Murphy, or Bill to my mother, and his Marine cut and long robe, which rumor had it concealed a weapon. And Terry, his young associate, with long kinky hair and a Texas drawl, who had counseled me once when I ran away from home. "Go home," he said. He never mentioned Jesus once.

Methodist, Peter said, sounding not very convinced of it.

"What are you looking for?" the kind priest asked us, glancing at my pudgy belly.

Short and sweet, I told him. Short and sweet.

Spencer Timothy MacLeod leapt into this world with a second good push at 2:30 in the morning, February 19th of 1980. As Peter cut the cord, Spencer was laid upon my chest looking like he just finished four rounds in the ring, his nose pushed to the side. I put my arms around him, becoming *mother,* and I instinctively knew I was made for this. For the first time in a very long time, maybe ever, I knew I had done something completely right. Just three days later, the US would upset the Russians at the Winter Olympics in New York, winning a gold in hockey – the "miracle on ice." But it paled in comparison to the miracle I held in my arms. He was all mine, and he had a look of perfect contentment on his face.

I laid him on the couch when I got home from the hospital, looked at this peculiar bundle that came with no directions, then knelt on the floor, resting my face an inch from his, his breath soft and shallow. Peter left for work, so the small cottage was quiet but for the steady wind outside.

It was hard to just let him be. The maternity nurse had showed me how to wrap him tight, like a burrito, so I lifted him easily to my shoulder and settled into the rocker. And we rocked together, our bodies now apart, but still conformed. *I did all right,* I thought. *Who would've guessed?* The little body curled into mine, the breath warm on my neck.

The chair swung softly back and forth, and outside the trees swayed in the winter wind, black on gray. It was a time of miracles, and for then, and for that time, nothing else mattered. *Spencer...* I pressed my face to his. *I will never let you go.*

The peepers returned, the osprey circled, heralding a new spring, and I watched the tall gray locust trees outside turn a pale shy yellow green, then open completely as the southern wind warmed the sandy earth. Peter worked on a scalloping boat out of Provincetown, ten days on and five days off, and as Spencer and I waved from the dock, we slipped into our rhythm of walks and naps and bumping down dirt roads in our VW bus through the backwoods of Truro, the motion rocking Spence to sleep. I didn't want to get drunk anymore. Motherhood was the missing piece – now life was complete.

But six months later, Peter nearly lost his life in a surprise nor'easter. Four local boats went down and when he came ashore, he kissed the ground and walked away from offshore fishing forever. So we turned to our own harbor and picked oysters, shucked oysters and sold them up and down the Cape, by the bushel or the quart. The Wellfleet oyster was famous all the way to the Grand Central Station Oyster Bar in New York City.

Walking the flats of Wellfleet harbor as the quahogs spit at your feet, with a rake and burlap bags in hand, or wading into the river as the tide drifted past brought an other-earthly peace to the soul. It was hard work; I carried 60-pound bags over my shoulder, in the sand, salt water running down my back into my waders and no man would rush to help. There was an unspoken code – if you couldn't handle it, you shouldn't be out there. We all walked head down and rarely spoke, because words didn't belong out there. Just an occasional nod, a quick Yankee smile connected us all to a place that was pure and timeless.

That winter, Cape Cod bay froze and we joined the ranks of the unemployed fishermen. The wine came out, most of it lifted from the local market. I had not lost my gift. And just when you thought you couldn't take one more night locked down from the fury of the squall that banged on the windows, it stopped. The wind changed direction and the ice floes broke up and beached. All it took was just one day edging up to the 40's for everyone to come out from under the covers, blinking in the sun, smiling like we're all in love.

The warm air dipping into the frigid bay brought a thick fog up the hill to our small house, brought oysters again and the pungent smell of last season's shells thawing in the back. The little boy was walking and talking. Time for a stroller. I threw him on my hip and walked into Bradlees, the nearest retail store 20 minutes away in Orleans.

We tried out every stroller on the floor, checking for comfort and good wheels for the Wellfleet dirt roads and of course a sun canopy. When I picked the right one, I plopped Spencer down in it and wheeled towards the door. I grabbed a sun hat off a rack, which I threw on my head, as we breezed past the cash registers into the lovely spring day. The sales clerks were as clueless as the little blond boy, so happy in his new free stroller.

CHAPTER 6

GOODBYE, HELLO

"Daddy has cancer," my mom informed me shortly after Spencer's birth. "Uncle Gerry says it looks bad." Gerry was her brother, a doctor. It always seemed to me that in my mom's family, everything looked bad, part of the Southern romance with tragedy. My grandfather and my uncle were both doctors, and I could see them shaking their heads and quietly landing the verdict. Esophageal cancer. Too bad.

My father began a journey through surgery, radiation and chemotherapy that was so violent back then, men would opt for death. It racked his large frame and quickly spent his reserve. He had been sober for seven years and remarried; at age 54, life was finally good. But the toll on his body from the treatment drained him of strength, and life slipped away slowly, disregarding his every hope and prayer, until that was gone too.

We had become friends, or at least come to a treaty of sorts. I expected an apology after he finally quit drinking, when he took inventory and measured the wreckage. Once, over lunch on his rooftop in Manhattan, I steered the conversation past old injuries, prodding for repentance. I re-dug one of my best hurts – violent and ugly. His fork stopped in midair, macaroni salad falling as he gestured.

"I never did that," he said flatly. We locked eyes, two seconds was all I could bear. It would never come, what I wanted most. *I'm sorry Rob. Forgive me, my little girl.*

As he became sicker I visited New York more often with his only grandson. Grandpa was smitten with the blond toddler with blue eyes like his. If there was anything my dad was a natural at, it was acting like a kid, and the visits seemed to transform him. In August of 1981 I announced I was pregnant again, due in April of the next year.

"Oh that's *great,* Bird," he said, mustering enthusiasm, but I could feel the weariness in his voice. He was not making ground.

We wrote often that fall, safer with words on paper. My letters were filled with the desolate beauty of the Cape after the rush of summer tourism had folded up its beach chairs and boarded the windows. Nor'easters pounded the dunes, seagulls pressed against the wind, flying backwards. He liked that, that even though they weren't going anywhere, they kept flying.

December 9th, my brother Bob called early.

"Dad's in the hospital." He paused making sure I was there.

"Okay."

"They think he might not make it."

"I'm on my way."

I wrapped my pregnant body into a thrift-shop mink and sped off in my VW beetle. The whole way down, the sky was the same gray color, through the mill towns of New Bedford and Fall River, through New London, where my father would always make us get out of the car and board a cramped World War II submarine that smelled like dirty socks. To him it was Disney.

Somewhere around New Haven I looked up at the thick winter sky. Seagulls flew aimlessly past the billboards, the tired Christmas shoppers, the endless traffic. I knew he was gone. I had missed it.

Riding up the escalator at Memorial Sloan Kettering in New York, I could see Bob's worried face ducking around the crowds, searching for his little sister. Finally our eyes met.

"He died, Robin." We cried in the lobby holding each other, next to a towering Christmas tree. Later a kind woman gave me tissues and I realized that lots of people were crying and holding tissues and each other because it was a cancer hospital, and my dad wasn't the only one who lost that day. Still, he was gone. Again.

Miles Peter MacLeod entered the world April 22nd 1982, ready or not. My father's death and a marriage that was fragile and frayed left me exhausted, even before labor began. As I held this new baby boy in my hands, I noticed Miles looked tired too, and when he was awake, he had a way of turning up his eyebrows, as if he had a question. It might've been, "Do you guys know what you're doing?" I stayed the night, then we drove home in the front of our red Chevy pick-up.

My mother moved to Wellfleet when I was pregnant, a month before my dad died, selling the "big house" in Connecticut. I found her a large two-story apartment overlooking the harbor. My father, who had veered clear of mentioning my mother's name and was too sick to notice most things, issued a firm warning a few months before he died.

"Don't move your mother close by," he said, plain and clear. But I pictured grandma doing crafts with the kids while the cookies browned in the oven. Or maybe just letting them wreck the house while she sat by a window.

"I'm not babysitting." This announcement came about a week before Miles was due. "I raised five children," she said, "and I've done my time." She had this funny defiant stance she'd take when she was preparing for a fight, one foot forward and two fists back, like she was winding up to slug me.

But she had yielded to a night with Spencer while I gave birth to his brother, and was standing at the end of the driveway, watching for the truck, while Spence rode his three-wheeler in circles.

Milk crates filled with oysters were stacked against the side of the house, waiting for me to deliver them. Spencer followed me into the house and watched me lay Miles in the crib.

"Here's your new brother!" I said, trying to sound optimistic.

He stared silently at the bundle of blankets with a fuzzy head stuck out of the top. Miles blinked as the brothers eyed each other, Miles still looking worried. Spence put his head on my shoulder, and I drew him close. Then I walked out of the house, past a large pile of wood that I could hide behind. There I could cry.

CHAPTER 7

BECOMING 'FLEETIAN

I f you lived in Wellfleet for a whole year you would notice a few things. First, there was always a reason to drink. You drank in the summer to party and celebrate; the beach, the bars, cars stuffed with young people unwinding from college, fisherman with full nets. Restaurants and cottage colonies were thronged with psychiatrists from New York paying top dollar for their vacation, for traffic and lines and the elusive *rest*. Cheers.

Then it was Labor Day and everything was shut down and rolled away like a huge carnival. You could stand at one end of Main Street and hear a leaf blow across the street at the other end. So you drank to celebrate having money and the Cape to yourself again.

In winter we drank through the long nights and the icy days in smoky bars telling stories of the harbor freezing over and when Pokey Snow got so drunk he drove his truck across the ice to Plymouth. We talked in poetry and unfinished dreams. Then when the peepers called up from the marsh, when the crocus burst through the crusted sand, it was spring finally – time to celebrate that winter was over.

The other thing you would notice is the large population of single mothers, colonies of them with the peculiar Wellfleetian style, also known throughout the Cape as "Fleetian." They wore their hair loose and long, clothes were a mish-mash of thrift-shop/hippie/homemade and there was an artsy, salty air about them. They reminded me of my New York City friends when I lived in the East Village. In New York you had to be tough just to navigate past the catcalls, the panhandlers and scammers. Here required a different resilience; to weather the gale, the bills, the bottle and missing men – and juggle little sea orphans with the other hand. Housing, food stamps, a check, and maybe a boyfriend that could fix stuff, helped.

Looking back, my marriage was not a bad one. But the normal pressures of parenting, survival and having to grow up began to break it down, slowly, like a neglected house. There were signs, there was warning, but no one, including us, did anything to stop the deterioration. In the fall of '83, it collapsed completely, and I joined the 'Fleetian single mom corps.

I moved into the upstairs of a barn, a little blond boy in each hand. The abutting house, a large white Victorian, housed three single moms with children and two single men – ex-husbands, drunken casualties. Both men died young; one hanged himself a few years later and the other fell overboard on a boat after an argument over a card game, too drunk to swim.

Men are jerks, I thought. I would stop by my mother's apartment with the boys and a bottle of wine and we would drink and laugh about them. I joined a women's steel drum band and even tried a women's support group where we could talk openly about our contempt towards men, but the truth was I still liked them.

As the winter drew near, I learned how to shuck scallops and Charles, a Frenchman with a black beret, dropped bags of bay scallops in the driveway.

"Eat as much as you want," he would say with a lovely accent, and a nod towards the burlap bags, and we did. Scallop curry, scallop scampi, scallop casserole, fried scallops, raw scallops. As I stood in the back yard over a big metal garbage can to one side and a make shift shucking table to the other, my raw hands worked the little knife until the rhythm of *Cut, Pull, Scrape* became as natural as my breath. Miles would play around my feet, sliding in the stray scallop guts until he grew tired, then he would hug my legs and cry. *Cut, Pull, Scrape…* the shells flew into the can and slowly the bucket filled with income.

At night the sherry came out, and I could feel the sharp edge of exhaustion ebb as the boys bounced around the small apartment until I lassoed them into bed. Often Spence would break Miles out of his crib in the middle of the night by unscrewing the rails, and I would awaken with a blurry awareness of two boys running loose, until I threatened them back to sleep.

"Quiet! We're in the library!" I yelled at the boys. It didn't matter. Books were flying off the shelves faster than I could catch them, and I could hear pages rip as they "read" a book of interest, usually the ones with the pull-tabs.

We walked to the library almost every day. It was the last stop of our routine trip to town; the post office, the donut shop or a blueberry muffin at the Lighthouse restaurant, then the library. It was more of a social stroll than errands. There was no mail delivery in Wellfleet then, so going to the Post Office to pick up your mail meant passing almost every citizen in town. It was a chance to catch up, to break through the cabin fever and to get all the news. Everyone knew everyone and their dog too.

The librarian looked like she was typecast; soft brown hair streaked with gray swept into a bun, spectacles, the colorless cardigan and A-line skirt with thick nylons and sensible shoes. I could see her out of the corner of my eye as I wrestled my sons, grabbing two books while I shoved the rest back wherever I could, hiding the torn pages. Her eyebrows were raised, as she peered over her glasses and leaned across her desk, like she was preparing to give a speech. But she never said a word. Even when I dropped the books off, pages sticky, torn or missing, she would say nothing.

Right before Christmas that first year, I pulled into the driveway with the boys in the pickup and saw the librarian at the top of my stairs, which climbed up the side of the barn. I frowned as I watched her face freeze with fear, then sprint down the stairs, the wind catching her long skirt. I thought she was going to yell at me about the torn books, and maybe rip up my library card, but she ran past me to her car parked on the street and drove off.

There, at the top of the stairs, was a brown shopping bag, and as we peeked inside, we all shouted, "Christmas presents!" Two large boxes were neatly wrapped with a note, *From the Congregational Church of Wellfleet. Merry Christmas!*

Inside, the boys tore open the boxes and lifted up two sets of pajamas with plaid bathrobes. I can't explain it, but that night, as I sipped my sherry and looked at them with the new jammies and robes on, and thought of the terrified librarian, I felt something like hope. It was fleeting, but it was something I knew I would not forget.

CHAPTER 8

TRAINS, PLANES AND A BRIDGE TO NOWHERE

*"If you don't know where you are going
any road can take you there"*

– LEWIS CARROLL, *ALICE IN WONDERLAND*

That summer, I boarded a bus for Charleston, South Carolina. Marian had detected my exhaustion and asked me to come stay with them on Edisto and cook for J.G. while she took a tour of Mexico with her daughter. The boys ran up and down the bus aisle all night long. The Benadryl that the pediatrician recommended for the ride had a reverse effect, causing them to ricochet off of each other and the narrow confines of the dirty bus.

The party in the back went on until 4 a.m. when the booze ran out and the loud laughter became weak and empty, then we all slept. As the lights flashed through the window, I held the two sweaty little boys, and hoped things would get better. I had not much to leave on Cape Cod – just a confusing mess, like a big junk drawer. *Richmond, Fayetteville.* The drunks snored; the boys were elbows and knees in the seat beside me as the sky grew lighter. *Pedro says South of the Border 50 miles.*

I watched the light play across their beautiful faces, and I was captivated by their peaceful expression. *They trust me. Amazing.*

We pulled into Charleston at midday. The bus floor was covered with something sticky and we smelled like a big ashtray. Marian looked alarmed when she saw us and I was suddenly aware that all three of us were filthy. J.G silently loaded our bags into the car, gently jesting with the boys.

I was hoping Edisto would bring what I needed, but that answer was elusive to me. It had been eight years, two children, a marriage and divorce later.

"There's been a lot of water under the bridge," Marian said, as we drove out to the island. Her voice alone seemed to release something inside that was stuck. It was May; the magnolias were in full bloom along with the blaze of magenta azaleas. The marsh air filled the car, the smell bringing healing, like a mother's hand to a fevered brow.

I loved going to church on Edisto, but it never crossed my mind on the Cape. I had grown up visiting the old pre–Civil War church, running between the crumbling grave markers and the massive live oaks, draped like old spinsters in Spanish moss.

No one in the church was younger than 50 and they all shopped at Dillard's. I think what I loved the most was the way we would linger afterwards, like God had pulled everyone up on his lap. Marian introduced me as "cousin," and they embraced me, the Yankee girl with the frown and faded t-shirts. My boys were little blond dust devils, whirling and smashing through the crowd, tumbling out into the graveyard where they could play hide and seek. A kind woman gave me new shoelaces for their sneakers and I thanked her, but I didn't see why you'd replace laces that worked just fine even if they'd been broken and retied into dirty knots several times.

Charles Spencer was a retired preacher that lived down the creek from Marian and J.G. and was married to J.G.'s sister. His name inspired my son's name. Even at 70 he could catch a Frisbee. Thin and slightly bent, at over six feet he was all limbs and walked with a bounce. I never saw him not smiling or laughing, something that grated on J.G.'s appreciation for silence or an occasional serious conversation.

One day sitting on Charles' porch, I asked him if he would baptize my boys. He laughed and told me, "Don't worry, if they died they would go to heaven!"

I hadn't thought of that, although J.G. had mentioned that he saw alligator tracks in his yard, so I might want to take the boys swimming in the ocean instead of the creek. I watched them chase each other in the shade of a huge magnolia. Charles studied them with a wide grin. He had fathered three boys.

"What you want to think about is, do you want to become a part of Christ's family." He paused and kept looking towards the marsh. "When you're ready for that, you can all be baptized." I looked away before he could catch my eyes. I was not ready, that's all I knew.

Several days later, he stopped by with a little booklet for me, the Gospel of John, and a note tucked inside. "To read at your leisure – Charles." I placed it on my bed and stared at it, feeling my face flush, unable to name what I felt.

I began a habit of borrowing Marian's car, telling J.G. I was "taking a ride" every evening. The one liquor store on the island was my first stop. With two or three little bourbon nips in my pocket, I could unwind, stopping by the beach or the pier to let the boys run. Their skin had turned brown as a pecan in the June sun, and their hair white. As I sipped the warm bourbon and watched them jump the small waves, I knew it was time to head north soon.

J.G. had suffered from headaches that summer that soon would evolve into several small strokes, signaling the onset of dementia. He also suffered through my cooking and scream-ing, so we parted with mutual gladness. I had pushed him away, sensing an undercurrent of distrust. On a small island, his wife's car frequenting the liquor store must have circled back to him quickly. He was known as the Judge, a fair man, with a keen sense of smell for trouble.

On the way to the train, he handed me a wad of money, nodding, and I took it. We said goodbye and he moved to hug me, but I turned and waved, and he looked relieved. Once on the Amtrak, I settled us into our seats and took out my Very Fine Apple juice, filled to the cap with Jack Daniels.

I forgot I had no home. Wellfleet in the summer was prime real estate, and bodies were shoved into every corner.

I had lost my apartment at the Single Mothers Manse – something about being a slob. My mother caved in and let us stay with her for two long nights, then a fisherman friend who had recently moved to Alaska asked me to visit. He was making boatloads of money on salmon and cocaine. If I liked it, I could stay and become rich too. A week later, we were gone.

Alaska is far from Cape Cod. Alaska is far from everywhere, even Seattle. As we flew over the teal-green mountains that wound endlessly through British Columbia and the Yukon Territory it occurred to me that nothing much had changed out here since the glaciers settled in.

The mountains grew taller with white caps as we approached Anchorage, then landed. In the airport, an enormous stuffed polar bear waved to the boys and they waved back, spinning with excitement as we made our way to the final flight. It was a small twelve-seater, and the pilot moved us around to distribute the weight evenly. Then he took off, it appeared at first, straight into the side of a massive mountain, suddenly twisting to the right and flying around it. A half hour later, we reached our final destination, Cordova. As the plane jerked to a stop, I looked out at the mist and tall pines and my heart hit my feet. It was the loneliest place I had ever seen.

Years later, Spence and Miles loved to tell their friends that we lived in Alaska.

"Didn't we Mom?" they would cue me, with the friend smiling in disbelief.

"Oh yeah. We sure did," I would answer. Six weeks in an 8-foot trailer next to a mountain on a road to nowhere. Well, it went somewhere. Fifty miles out of town to a massive expansion bridge that collapsed during an earthquake in 1964. You could stop and look at the glaciers; some liked to shoot at them hoping to break off a piece and watch it crash into the Copper River with a sound like a cannon. Then you had to get back in your truck and drive home.

My fisherman friend was not there. He was off making money. So our days, which were really long because it was August and the sun set briefly at about midnight then popped back up again an hour later, were loosely filled with figuring out how to fill long days in Alaska. For two small boys, it was heaven. For me, pretty close to hell.

The town of Cordova was built on the side of a mountain, overlooking Prince William Sound. Every store sold booze, even ice cream parlors, and there were passed out Indians and fat white women everywhere. Alaskans were friendly enough, nicer than I could be. But the mountains bothered me, more and more each day, like they were slowly moving in on me, and taking away the sky, my escape.

The boys would get covered in dark glacier dust that kicked up with any movement, sticking to their hair and hands. I would try to wash them with our dishes in a nearby mountain stream but eventually I had to take them to the community pool for a full rinse.

In the evening, I would sip on a pint of bourbon and hang towels across the small windows, darkening our home to entice sleep. Spencer would set "bear traps," using rope and several five gallon buckets. It was doubtful he would catch a bear I thought, watching him each night, but he could possibly trip one that was lumbering through our camp.

We never did see a bear; just bear poop – or a moose, which still makes me sad.

After two weeks, I called my mother, crying and depressed, begging for a bailout. She declined. Eventually my fisherman friend returned and kindly sent me home.

I caught strep throat and Miles picked up impetigo from the community pool right before we departed – a fitting bon voyage. He used an old slip of mine as his "silky" and on the flight home, he took to tossing it over the seats. It was filthy, covered in glacier dust and snot, which poured from his nose that was crusted with impetigo sores. An elderly woman told me to wipe my kid's nose. My throat felt like it was lined with glass shards and I was racked with fever. As the plane pressed eastward, I hoped to forget Alaska, like a disturbing dream that dissipates quickly when you wake up and think of other things.

Mom! Tell 'em we lived in Alaska, they'd say for years to come when friends came over.

Yes, we sure did. They never let me forget it.

We were still homeless, renting a room week to week with a mattress on the floor from a friend in town. Then an apartment opened up, with two bedrooms, and we were giddy with the space and luxury of two beds, even if the roof leaked into our kitchen and the front yard was a patch of dirt. There was a beautiful manicured yard on the side of the house but the landlord said it was only for his kids to play on. The whole year we were there I only saw one kid, a chubby sullen boy who kicked a ball in circles through the thick green grass by himself.

At night, we would play *Bar.* I was the customer, the one with a large bottle of vodka and a glass. Spence and Miles would make snacks, pulling food from the fridge and chairs to the counters as rock and roll blasted through the small apartment. I was a happy customer, pouring my self another one as the boys ran back and forth with saltine crackers and orange government cheese on a plate. I would leave about an inch in the bottle after last call, and we would all find our way to our beds, worn out in different ways, and sleep.

CHAPTER 9

TWO BOYS, TWO BIKES AND MY LAST HANGOVER

I took a job driving a school bus for Head Start, where both boys attended. Hung-over and cranky every morning, I laughed watching the kids fly out of their seats as I sent the school bus bouncing over the back roads of Wellfleet. The grand finale was the bridge to Lieutenant's Island, small and arched, enough to get air with enough speed.

"Here it comes! Hold on!" I'd yell.

"Whoa!" they screamed in unison, laughing as they jostled against each other and the sides of the small bus.

A couple of the moms were born-again Christians and I avoided them if I could.

"Jesus loves you!" they would say, smiling their goofy grins as their kids boarded the bus and I shut the door fast behind them.

I also shucked scallops for one of their husbands, and they would corner me in the garage, asking questions about my life. I seemed to have no good answers that would deter them from praying for me and I cringed when they put their hands on me as I stood there in the cold with a cigarette sticking out of my mouth and a shucking knife in my hand. We bowed our heads respectfully as they began praying, but I was looking at the bottle of sherry on the cement floor and the scallop guts on my boots, hoping they would hurry up.

My boyfriend, Tony, was good at fixing things, everything from my camera to my truck. Since a lot of things were broken, he stuck around. But as the Cape turned over, getting ready to hibernate through another winter, I was becoming undone. I did not want to party, I wanted to be left alone, in my home, with my vodka. I wanted to play bar, but the game was consuming me.

My doctor felt around my abdomen.

"Right here is where it hurts," I said, putting my hand over the upper right. "And it feels swollen too."

He stood up and looked at me briefly, then turned his back. "It's your liver," he said flatly. "Do you drink?"

"Some," I said. He turned back around.

"You shouldn't," he paused. "Not if you want to live." Then he left.

The silence of the empty room felt heavy and stupid. My head hurt and I wished I never came. I thought of my dad.

I had been forgetting things – like putting the boys to bed, putting myself to bed. I woke up with my head on fire, looking around for the boys, always amazed to find them asleep, like they were supposed to be. But I couldn't remember how they got there. I felt like one of my brother's marionette puppets that he used to play with when we were kids. One was a clown called Bobo and you could make Bobo do any silly thing you wanted by pulling his strings; kick himself in the head, smack his face with his hand. I was stupid Bobo and something had my strings. I was trapped, and like any trapped animal I felt powerless to get free. So I waited.

My first Parent-Teacher conference was with Spencer's kindergarten teacher, Mrs. Croteau. She was just as nice as you'd expect a kindergarten teacher to be, a little out of place in a town like Wellfleet with her Lands End sweater, wool skirt and knee socks. Her hair was neat and styled to flip under, and her eyes were sincere.

Tony had some cocaine so I snorted a line before my conference, and Mrs. Croteau and I had a great talk. I felt like Spencer's time in kindergarten was probably the most important thing in life, his life anyway, and by the time I left, I felt as if his teacher finally realized how intense my involvement and concern was for my child. We had, together, steered him onto a track of enlightened success; no mountain was too high, no road too hard for my son.

When I got home, I looked in the mirror and saw a big rock of cocaine hanging out of my nose.

My brother Bob quit drinking that September. My mother, without invitation, had arrived at the dirty room he was renting in Dorchester. She knelt at his bed and bent down to his face and said,

"I don't want to lose another son."

It was uncharacteristic for her, to get so close, to love impulsively. It was a risk and it worked. He found an AA meeting and he was now three months sober. I had invited him down for the weekend. It was December 29th 1985.

December 29th. I don't know why this date stuck, because I never got a chip or token, but it did. My memory of that day begins with a hangover, the kind that feels like your brains are pushing your eyeballs out of your head and your legs are someone else's. Two boys and their bicycles and a red pickup truck. It was cold and it didn't help that the parking lot ended at a steep sand dune, then the ocean, battle ship gray and angry, sending a vicious wind across the pavement that went right to your marrow. I doubt I felt the cold as I watched the two little blond heads circling on their bikes, yelling to each other, one age five on his two-wheeler and the three year old on the Big Wheels, spinning out in the sand.

It's hard to describe what happened that day, the day God interrupted my hangover and shook me by the shoulders. I know His voice came from inside but I was looking up, to the gray sky that became the ocean, then the sky opened up like a window and God leaned out: "You will be dead in six months if you don't stop drinking!"

It was just like that. I don't think I even considered being sober until that very moment even though I knew that I was dying inside, deep in my soul, like I was stuck in a sink hole and it was slow, awfully slow but I couldn't get free. I was tired, I was becoming what I thought I'd never be – my father, a drunk and like him, I was dying and I couldn't stop it.

The window shut and the sky seemed dense and silent but the words echoed within my throbbing head. I studied the two little boys again as they spun around the empty lot. No more me, no more mom. They needed a mom. How selfish to take that from them.

God, help me live. It was a weak plea. I never thought once that I could stop on my own.

I met my brother as he stepped off the Greyhound bus onto Main St. and I told him what had happened, and that I wanted to quit too. He looked frail and uncertain about both of us, but he was different, like he wasn't hiding anymore. He had finally found a place to anchor and I wanted that too. He told me to drink lots of Diet Coke and I wobbled across the finish line of 1985, having no idea how much I would have to celebrate someday.

I can't explain how it happened but I did not drink again – or smoke pot or take any other drug into my poor ravaged body. I recovered and two years later I met Jesus Christ, who introduced me personally to the same God who graciously reached down into the thick deep mud of my life that cold winter day and pulled me out.

CHAPTER 10

RUNNING INTO JESUS

November 1987

I had every intention of going to school that night. I was taking courses at the local community college, slowly pursuing my nursing degree. But at the bottom of the ramp off of the highway, I turned left instead of right. I pulled into the parking lot of a storefront church called Victory Chapel. It was packed. After months of being hounded by the Jesus girls in Wellfleet, curiosity got me, and I walked through the doors, finding Donna, the scallop guy's wife. The shock dissolved into a smile as she made room for me.

I didn't like it. The music was so corny and the guest preacher had a Texas twang. I still can't recall a thing he said but this:

Who came here tonight looking for Jesus?

I remember because everyone had their heads bowed and it was almost over, the whole service and then I could leave, but instead I raised my hand, surprising myself, then reasoned: *Well, yes, I suppose I am a little curious, that's all.*

Then he asked me to get up and go down to the altar, so I did, embarrassed but grateful to be with several others heading to the floor with me.

A young girl asked me to repeat a prayer, asking God for forgiveness and to receive Jesus as my Lord and Savior, but I don't think she had to do that. God had already met me there, on that thin, shabby carpet and was doing a heart transplant. When I stood up, a bunch of Wellfleetians stood around me in a semi-circle, with goofy grins looking like they were going to cry. I felt like I was in one of those dreams where you forget to put pants on, so I turned and left, saying nothing. Relieved to get outside, I ran to my old Ford window van, jumped inside and spun off.

What happened? I wondered as I made my way to the highway. I needed to figure this out. The stars were brilliant, and seemed to spin and twirl in the black night. I wanted to laugh, but this was serious. What happened to me? I drove on in silence, alone with my thoughts, but aware that something was very different.

You need to forgive your father.

The words were so clear, I checked my rearview mirror for a voice, but I knew that the Voice was not a person. I had heard that voice before, in a parking lot almost two years before.

I did. We made amends, I argued. My dad had died seven years ago; we were friends. Besides, he's long gone now. Silence. I felt foolish all of a sudden. My argument was shallow and a lie.

Forgive your father. Again, a gentle but unrelenting press deep within me.

Ok, yes, I forgive my father. The press released and instantly

I was flooded with a torrent of joy so magnificent I could hardly hold the steering wheel. I did laugh out loud. As I pulled into the driveway and shut off the engine, my darkened house looked different. Everything looked different, and as I crawled into bed that night, I did not need to understand it all, I just knew I never wanted to lose it.

In the morning, the sun peeled back another day and as I heard the thump of little boy feet hitting the floor, my eyes shot open. *Is he still here? God, or was it Jesus? The One who met me on my knees, the One who drove home with me.*

As my mind jumped back to the night before, I lay still, waiting, then smiled.

Yes, the Voice spoke. *Still here.*

I didn't know it then, but I had just been born again.

That same week, standing in line at a checkout counter, I reached for a pack of cigarettes that were neatly stacked above the magazines, and strained from my peripheral vision for any onlookers. I paused, making sure I was clear. I'd done this so many times, it was natural as scratching an itch. I grabbed the pack, got ready to swing around and pretend I had dropped something, then bend down and whoosh! slam-dunk the butts in the bag. But out of nowhere, fear gripped me by the back of the neck and shook me. I could feel my face burn red and I quickly threw the Marlboro's back up on the display. Being scared was as good as being caught – that much I knew. Then I smiled. I really was changed.

Someone was always watching me now, Someone who cared.

CHAPTER 11

THE THING ABOUT CHURCH

*We now have this light shining in our hearts,
but we ourselves are like fragile clay jars
containing this great treasure. This makes it
clear that our great power is from God, not
from ourselves.*

– 2ND CORINTHIANS 4:7 NLT

In the book of Hosea, God commands the prophet Hosea to stick with his adulteress wife named Gomer. She has not just slipped and had a one-night stand, but cheats on him over and over again like it's no different than a shopping spree. The Bible calls her a whore, but God is unwavering with Hosea. He must stay with her; and he must go back for her again and again.

What makes the story extra painful is that you can sense Hosea's love for her, and her indifference towards him. Although this initially depicts God's love for Israel, it is a foreshadowing of Christ and His church. We are Gomer. It's humbling at the very least, but should also point us to God's magnificent mercy and fierce love.

This was always a comfort to me, because for about five years I felt like a beggar among royalty. I knew I needed a home, a family to love me but I had nothing to offer. I was unlovely. I struggled with the corpse that kept trying to rise again, to reclaim the new Robin that Jesus had birthed, pure and dumb as fresh dirt.

The first church I found was a small charismatic church meeting in a movie theatre in Wellfleet. The pastor was a big jovial man who loved to sing and laugh loud and his wife was a stunning woman with big frosted hair and jewelry that matched her dresses. If you asked her how she was, she quoted scripture from the Amplified Bible. And since I knew nothing, I would just stare at her, gawking like a half-wit, wishing I could at least comeback with some King James. They passed popcorn buckets for the offering and gave out goldfish for communion.

I was pure Wellfleetian – I didn't own a bra and had a pair of flip-flops for shoes. My hair was just one style -- long and tangled and the only time I ever wore lipstick was when I was six and ransacked my mother's vanity drawer. I did not care about what God could give me; I just wanted to not get thrown out. The pastor called me "Blessing."

A lot of what the church people did grated on me. I sat in the front row with my arms folded, despising how they all smiled and clapped and sang like we were in a musical. I was trying to quit smoking so I chewed on lollypops and slouched down low in my seat, scowling.

The song leader was a fierce-looking black woman from Dorchester, a city girl, with a voice from the throne of God.

One Sunday she frowned at me from the platform and right in the middle of a song yelled, "Get up and clap!" I jumped to my feet and I clapped, almost choking on my lollypop.

In time I grew to love the songs that seemed so corny at first. My pastor's joy was infectious as he sang and when we stopped singing songs, we would sing "in the spirit," eyes closed and hands lifted. More than once I had to peek and open my eyes a little because I could swear I heard angels singing with us. I wept, unsure if the source was pain or joy – it didn't really matter. God was touching places deep in my soul that had been dark and dormant for years.

Before Halloween, they announced that we don't believe in Halloween, because it's the devil's holiday so instead we would have a "Hallelujah Party" and every one could dress up as a Bible character. I was fuming – it seemed ridiculous, maybe even cultish. So I took the boys out trick or treating early, then came home and dressed them as Bible characters; the devil and a snake. The pastor's mouth opened just a little when we came through the door, then he caught himself and smiled.

"Hello Blessing!"

Tony and I married after living together for two years. I wanted to make things right, but it was wrong, I knew it was wrong. I remember driving through the White Mountains on our honeymoon and staring out of the car window at nothing, my gut twisting, my eyes tired and aching. *I do* meant forever. Still, I thought, if God could rescue me, He could get anyone. I held on to that. And I knew that church was what I needed, every time I could get in the door. So we went, the whole bunch of us, including Tony's six-year-old daughter Sadie, who moved in with us.

Somehow, I understood a few important things, and early on. I learned to shut up and listen, that my opinion wasn't very weighty in God's kingdom. I learned I had a lot to learn and there was a boatload of grace in God's classroom. And I learned to serve, that Jesus puts His hands over ours when we put our hands to work. The first official service we had, the pastor's wife came up to me in a panic and asked if I could teach the kids in Sunday School. *Sure*, I said. All I remember is Jesus, Love and lots of Goldfish.

Then they asked me to play piano. *Sure.* I had bought a $50 upright piano and painted it turquoise, secretly learning the Jesus songs so I could sing at home. My fingers were stiff and clumsy. After my brother died, I took piano lessons and the little girl who couldn't sit still for five seconds was transformed on a hard piano bench. There was a language beyond the 16th notes on the page that released me from the deafening silence that seized my home. Bach and Beethoven were my best friends. But at age twelve I started to run away, and at fifteen I left them and my home for good.

I stopped playing for 17 years.

Poor Mrs. Adams, my teacher, learned my first recital that my stage fright was crippling. Now, in church, it was so bad my hands bounced on the keys like I was having a seizure. Then the exiting keyboard player gave me some simple advice: play like no one is in the room except Jesus. After that, I would picture Him sitting there in a big empty room with His arms folded, leaning back comfortably in the seat with a big smile on His face as I tripped and stumbled up and down the keys.

"That's my Robin," He would say, trying not to laugh.

Spence and Miles joined a Christian rap and dance band in the church called Triple Play. Our whole church had about 30 people in it but three were teenagers that had a zeal and passion to serve God, which could easily slide into just zeal and passion at their age. Often members of the band would get ejected for different infractions, but most of it had to do with girls. Spence was no exception. But the boys kept pressing in, putting down roots that would bear fruit down the road. It gave practical understanding to the cost of living for Jesus. Our lives, together and individually, were no longer our own.

I changed. As the Potter gently worked the clay, layers of defiance and rebellion peeled away. I found beauty in submission, peace in humility. That God could love me, just as I was, took a while to sink in. For a long time, I felt like I had snuck in the back door, that I could never be like them, the Real Christians, until I realized that none of us deserve grace, and that we were all Gomer, but God was faithful as long as we kept coming back, that when He looked at me, I was a beautiful bride, not a harlot. I was "Blessing."

CHAPTER 12

EXODUS

Manna:
- the substance miraculously supplied as food for the Israelites in the wilderness
- an unexpected or gratuitous benefit

Fall 1994

The divorce mediator left the small room with a stack of paperwork to copy and I tried to slow down my breath. Tony sat beside me, strangely close after a year of being apart. He had left when our son, Jacob, was a year and a half, too young to even know his dad was gone forever.

Jake was my happiest baby, the big green eyes, the little round face searching mine, waiting for a smile. It was a spark of light in the turmoil of a home tearing apart, oblivious joy in the face of defeat. Five years of pushing my faith past the grim reality of a gangrenous marriage, pushing past the fear - wanting to know truth, but afraid of finding it: Jacob stood in the middle of it, insisting that Spence, Miles and I laugh. His world was a party.

I knew I had to forgive, to release the whole mess – and as I sat next to the strange man I had lived with for seven years, I felt sorry for him, not pity but sad that he missed it, the Joy. I knew God still loved him, so I could too. Healing would take time, but I was free from the snare of bitterness.

Tony and I signed some papers and made a brief appearance before a judge who had nothing to say but a few well-rehearsed lines about reasonable civility. I felt bad for him, spending the whole day banging his gavel like a death knell every time a marriage died. As I pushed the heavy double door open and stepped out of the Probate court into the chill of a damp fall morning, I thought, *It's over*. I did not feel sad or glad, just an awareness of a season ending, and a new one before me. I took in a deep breath and looked upward.

I don't know why God asks us to stand and fight for things that He knows won't work in the long run, and I struggled with that a lot at first. Where was the take-away? My family had shipwrecked; we were refugees in a barren land, foraging for survival. Sadie left to go live with her mom. Spencer, at age 13, was slipping away from me into places that were dark and hidden, and Miles, the quiet, undemanding child, was spending too much time alone.

My church shut down too. I didn't know that you could do that – just leave, but it happens. We never grew, and a church needs money, so the pastor from Boston who was supporting our church came down and told us he was "pulling the plug." It was a good metaphor because some of us did just die. Others went off and breathed on their own for a while, languishing on TV evangelism or cerebral books. I knew I had to find a new church or I would die too.

The new Baptist church was nice. It had a big steeple and a large colorful nursery with expensive toys. The pastor was a thin, nervous looking man who talked like he already knew the people wouldn't believe a thing he said, and I noticed the people on the left side of the aisle clapped and raised their hands, and the people on the right didn't. *So it's not perfect,* I reasoned. After they announced that the Youth group had pizza on Thursdays, I was all in. But as I pulled out of the parking lot, I felt God say, "Not here."

The next Sunday, we were all sitting in the sanctuary of a little church that had just gone through a big split. So since it was small to begin with, that left them with about 13 people – 13 tired, cynical people. The pastor looked at me and said, "Can you play the keyboard?"

Sure.

There was no nursery, no youth group, no steeple, but God said, "Yep, this is it." So we stayed – Jacob breaking free and tripping down the aisles laughing, and Spence and Miles sitting in the back, slouched in their seats with arms folded, daring God to move them, while I banged on the keyboard from the front.

I made it a practice not to cry in front of my kids, although Miles told me years later that he walked into the kitchen behind me once when I was sitting at the table with bills spread out in front of me, weeping. He stepped quietly back, knowing I didn't want him to see me.

It wasn't so much pride. I just didn't want them to be scared. I mean, things looked bad: no husband, lots of bills, church packed up and gone, police at the door. But in the midst of all that, I think each one of us knew that God was there, and we knew it separately, personally, when we were alone; when Miles went down to the basketball courts to shoot hoops by himself, when Spence sat in the principal's office, when I cried over the bills. We knew, and we also knew we were not alone. And this made all the difference.

I can't remember now where I bought the board – a simple chalkboard that you would use in a restaurant to write Today's Specials on. But I do remember the first scripture I wrote on it:

The joy of the Lord is your strength. Nehemiah 8:10

It was an odd, out-of-place statement in my busted home – almost defiant. A single mom with a mountain of debt, two angry teens and a toddler living day to day on the tender grace of God. There was not much room for joy, but God made room and even supplied the joy Himself. His joy became my strength.

I remember my eyes catching the chalkboard as I walked into the kitchen, retracing the simple words, and allowing them to settle deep within. On different days, the meaning would shift, like a crystal turning in the sun, and His joy became mine. I caught hold of Hope and I could see it sifting down into the boys, turning the cynicism into wonder.

Eventually the verse changed and it became a family center-piece, the words surrounded by my very limited artistic scratch; some flowers crawling up the sides or leaves falling from a tree, then snow with an occasional bird, the same bird, showing up on a fence or branch. If I got too busy and neglected it, I would hear, "Mom, isn't it time to change the board?"

And I would watch with amusement as the older boys would pause and read the latest entry, as if the hand of God had penned it.

I could argue that indeed He did. Years later, when several of Spence and Miles' friends were worn out after hitting a wall on the streets or in jail, and I would point them to Jesus, I would hear: "I remember you had that chalkboard in your kitchen…"

I didn't know you had to ask for your dirt. Stepping out onto the back stoop, I surveyed my new yard. The new septic was paid for by the previous owner, and the whole back yard was torn up to accommodate it. What they left was sand. No dirt – they took the dirt, probably to sell, because on Cape Cod people pay for real dirt. Sand was hard to grow stuff in, although clover, sea grass and Rosa Rugosa loved it. I sighed, my eyes burning from the bright daylight. Rosa Rugosa… that's what I'll plant.

We had just moved into our first house we ever owned.

"This is ours," I told my boys. "Nobody can tell us what to do, or when to move anymore!" And with that, Miles passionately spray-painted his name in three-foot letters across the basement wall in Day-Glo orange.

We had left Orleans a few months earlier and moved to a small rental in Yarmouth. I thought the boys would be sad but they weren't. We had all been wounded in some way, or at least let down, but I think each of us carried a small amount of hope, fragile like a baby bird when you're not sure if it will live or not.

It was a small rental, it was a new start, and then the landlord showed up one month later and said we had to leave. I found a big tree in the back yard to hide behind and wept. Then I got the big idea to buy a house. I even told my kids, "You watch! God will turn this into something better!" Spencer laughed out loud. He was 14 and knew everything worth knowing. His mom was out of her mind.

Now I squinted into the sandy lot of our own little house. It looked like a throw back to the sixties – real wood paneling, a red and white-checkered linoleum floor in the kitchen. Rolling pins and canisters danced across the wallpaper, and the living room boasted an authentic orange shag carpet.

But I liked it.

It's ours! I thought. No more crazy landlords. *Thank you Lord*. And I meant it.

I wasn't so stupid to think that Spencer wouldn't drag trouble down here. In fact, the Yarmouth Police had already greeted us. A break in at the Little League concession stand. Several boys involved…Spencer and Miles' names came up. Boxes of candy bars had been confiscated from an apartment in Swan Pond Village, a low-income housing complex about a mile away. *Okay, officer, I'll bring them down.*

And so it starts.

But it was not all bad. God let me know that, it was impossible to deny it. A landlord in Orleans drops our rent, a credit card company cuts the bill in half, a lawyer never sends a bill. And smaller things… an old man drops a bag of clamshells every week so I can hammer out a shell driveway. Sandy and Steve, a couple from church, fix a bathroom sink, put together a swing set for Jake that came with 400 screws, put up a picket fence for my beach roses to lean against.

Sometimes when I drove away from the house at night, heading to work on the night shift, I could swear I saw an angel or two sitting on the roof. Seems crazy, but there was a lot that was crazy about those first years in the little Cape house on Geneva Rd.. Some things were scary, like when Spence came home from his first day of high school with a black eye and he would not tell me why. Then there was the broken nose and the night he came home with blood trailing from his head down his back. His friend Jermaine said someone hit him in the head with a folded chair "for no reason." He would not let me take him to the ER. It was his mouth, I knew it. My mother used to call me Last Word Lucy. Just got to say one last thing…

Miles was not much better. He was creating a reputation for himself in middle school. A fiery, scrappy boy with big clothes hanging on his thin frame; his attitude screamed at anyone in his way. He was gifted in basketball, fast and furious, but his mouth and temper were stealing the show. I couldn't bear to watch it and left the game more than once, wondering why a coach would accommodate that. He was making friends just like him too and the police were calling me for both boys. I scheduled their juvenile cases together if I could, catnapping in my car during court recess after working all night.

Fights erupted on a regular basis in our home. CD's and cigarettes were confiscated; posters of sneering rap stars were thrown out. One morning I dumped a case of empty beer bottles I discovered behind the fence on Spencer's floor, next to his bed.

"Rise and shine," I said, as he scrambled to his feet amid rolling brown bottles.

"Mom!" he yelled.

"If you don't like my rules, talk to Jesus," I would say. "He's in charge here."

Every morning three-year-old Jacob would get up smiling and put on his cowboy hat, or Batman cape and off we would go to daycare. Then I would fall into bed, asleep in seconds, setting my alarm for six hours later when I would pick him up. He was happy everyday, and his delight in both ordinary and imaginary things spread to us all and often pulled us together. It was if God was pointing to the simple faith of a small boy in the middle of a raging sea and suddenly the teenage turbulence and a single mom's fear became senseless. It was faith that he would be cared for, we would all be cared for, that every day was a new day and worthy of rejoicing in.

I had to believe in angels and a God who was much bigger than my small house with the big sand pit in the back, bigger than police and judges, a God who listened to the exhausted prayers of a scared mom.

It was time to go get Jacob. I stretched, fully awake and turned to go inside, but stopped, spotting a spray of color in the small dirt patch beside the house, *real dirt*, I thought. Flowers, they were actually growing. I walked over and looked closer. Zinnias. A bright red bud waved in the sun. Others would join it soon, maybe orange and some yellow too. I had planted in the late spring; well, more like threw some seeds at the dirt, then stepped on them. I smiled, turning back to the door. *Thanks Jesus.*

CHAPTER 13

POLICE, PRAYER AND A SURPRISE VISIT

"It was the blood, Jesus died to save the whole human race
all you thugs, hard rocks with hard looks on your face,
broken hearted, need a touch of
God's amazing grace.
There's a black cloud that follows you from the cradle to the
grave."

—SONG BY SPENCER MACLEOD '97

The new church we found was run by a sweet couple that let me cry on them a lot. Sometimes I'd play the piano and just weep. I knew Jesus cared, that He cared more deeply about Spencer than I ever could, but I felt like I was losing him, my grip weakening.

One day I asked the pastor if he would leave the church open for me so that I could go there after work and pray. The sanctuary was cool and quiet as I softly walked to the altar. I fell down on the steps, exhaustion taking over, and I wasn't sure what I could say. Or if it mattered.

God, the more I try, the worse it gets, I sobbed, my hot tears falling onto the carpet. I lay silent for what seemed a long time, overwhelmed by my failure. Then, with my eyes closed, I took my son and lifted him to God, to heaven and the army of angels I needed to rescue him. I placed him on the altar then stood, raising my hands to heaven, still weeping.

"He's yours, Father. I know You will care for him better than I ever can. I give him to you Jesus." And I stepped away, suddenly immersed in a warm wave of peace. I looked around. The room was still silent but there was Someone there.

"Thank You," I said, raising my hand to His, and I slowly turned, lighter now, and headed home.

Chuckie Peterson was a bright man I found out years later. But when I first heard his name from Spence and Miles, they were on a carousel of trouble, small stuff, and blaming the rest of the world for their own stupidity. "Chuckie" they called him with no reverence for his real name, Detective Peterson.

Mom, they would complain in tandem. *He has a five-o complex!*

This statement would precede a story in which they, my little thug sons, weren't doing *anything* wrong, and then suddenly he appears, sometimes with screeching tires, just like TV, leaping from his unmarked car, and roughing them up, sometimes throwing them against his car, and growling at them like a rabid pit bull.

I fell only once for their stories. This one involved the State Police, who had barracks right down the street from our house.

Mom, Spence said, *they really beat me up. They shouldn't be allowed to get away with that.* He looked so earnest.

Yeah, Mom, said his brother, who acted like a public defender too often. *They really hurt him.*

So I stopped in to talk to the troopers. I was mildly indignant. The trooper patiently heard my case.

"Spencer MacLeod?" he asked, not waiting for an answer while he turned to his computer. "Let's see what we have."

A minute later, the printer kicked in, and spit out a page, two pages. Then more. Thirteen pages later, I was getting up to go. I never listened to them again.

Spence quit school when he was fifteen.

"They liked me so much, they let me quit early," he would say years later with a smile. This was not devastating to me, because like Spence, I was so bored in high school I just never showed up most of the time, finally graduating six months late. I told him he had to work, to help out with the lawyer's bills so he found work washing dishes, but he still found time to get into more trouble.

By the spring of '96, there was serious talk of incarceration. A pot possession, a huge brawl in a state park, and an arrest made when he and a friend drove a stolen car in circles in a large parking lot in downtown Hyannis. The ride ended in a collision with a cement post while two cops looked on from a cruiser parked at the end of the lot. That incident racked up about six charges. My mother said she would come up for the hearing, "just in case."

My relationship with my mother was held together by disasters and tragedies. It was a little bit of that southern mystique; the calm acceptance of impending doom, the tacit nod to ruin and wreckage. It intertwined our lives like wisteria in a dark forest.

My mother's side came from a long line of crazy dreamers who drifted into the intercoastal waterway from Scotland, and ran aground on the pre- Civil War shores of Edisto Island, off of South Carolina. There the Murrays multiplied, becoming one of several prosperous planters on the island, cashing in on Sea Island Cotton, which was at one time world renown, exported immediately into the shops of the finest Paris couture.

But Murrays never made it big.

"We dreamed too much," my mother confessed. We weren't failures, just not Forbes.

I remember her at the kitchen window, in a small chair pulled up to a counter that ran beneath the double window, an ashtray holding a lit Parliament, smoke aimless and a cup of coffee with the red lipstick stains along the rim. I was in that house for ten years before I left, and that posture didn't change; her dark eyes turned to the backyard, seeing something but nothing, her expression a little sad always, eyebrows slightly arched like she was waiting for an answer, then annoyed when the stream of thought was broken in on.

"Get outside. It's a beautiful day," she'd say, even though it could be hailing. And she'd turn back to wherever she left off. After my sister was born, she put her right behind her coffee cup and ashtray. Cigarette, coffee, baby in her infant seat, turned just right so that she could look out of the window too.

I don't remember her ever hugging me and never thought it was odd. At night, when I was small, she would check on us before she turned out her light and went to bed. I would fake sleep and wait for her lips to kiss my forehead, soft as feathers. Then the house turned dark.

When I grew up and saw mothers hugging and holding their kids, I got mad. I blamed my mess on her coldness, on my father's drunkenness and on God for His indifference. But after I met Jesus I started to look at things different. Now I saw that it was painful for her, that love was too big to fathom, too risky, especially after already losing one child. Her own mother had abandoned her for a bottle of bourbon. Raised by black nannies, she was well fed, well dressed but not well loved – a skinny white girl with red hair and dark secrets locked in her heart. She knew she loved us, she knew she would choose death for any of our lives, but beyond that, there were few meeting places.

When my life was at its worst, like when I went into the nuthouse or my marriages broke apart, she would recede into the distance, and then show up when it seemed safe.

"I knew you were going through a tough time, Bird," she would explain, "so I left you alone for a while."

This was normal, retreating from each other's private pain and it was something I was trained to copy. But now I could see that we both had failed, so I began telling her I loved her, and started hugging her too. At first it was awkward, and she would stiffen and make fun of me. Then she started to say she loved me too. Eventually she returned my hugs with little pats on the back, her hands like little wings.

It bothered her that Spence was in so much trouble. It bothered her because she knew it hurt me and it confirmed what she knew – that the world was wicked and that none of us could escape. But she took the drive from New York anyway, knowing that his court cases were pending and that the outcome could mean Spence would be taken away.

She got out of the car wearing a black shiny money belt around her little waist, under her shirttail.

"Just in case," she said, patting it gently. I don't think all of her money would've made a difference; this wasn't West Africa where a slight of hand to a uniformed official could detour justice. But she believed in the power of cash.

That day, the day God came into my kitchen, was just an ordinary day. I plugged in the iron and flipped the small cabinet open in the kitchen, releasing the ironing board. It was one of my favorite things about that house in Yarmouth.

It was Sunday morning and the spring sun was reaching through the window across the kitchen table where my mother sat reading. We were going to church, and it would all be okay. I threw my green silk shirt over the ironing board.

The iron spit and hissed while big and small feet thumped across the floor upstairs.

I picked up the iron and worked it across the shirt. Then it came – I would say suddenly but it was so quiet, like a great cloud. It came over me and I could barely stand, but I felt not weighed down but lifted up in it and part of it. It made no sound but did I hear a faint otherworld chorus, a far-away song? My mind raced to identify something I had never felt before...then I looked up and heard my mother simply say:

"He's here." Her voice was soft and her face had a look of child-like wonder as we both stared into...the air.

The air in the kitchen. You can't see air but I could, it was vibrant and translucent, like it was doused in gold. I couldn't speak, I could just look and then I couldn't look any more. I wanted to laugh or shout but I couldn't make noise. I closed my eyes and bowed my head. Then it was gone. *Joy,* my mind

finally spoke. It was joy unspeakable, like the song we sang...
"and full of glory." Love had tipped the pitcher and let a few
drops of heaven, of God's own glory fall upon a tired single
mom and her skeptical mother.

For a long time I thought God did that for my mom.
It was fun to see her face light up, and the earnest way she
would tell people about how God came into my kitchen. The
cynic, the intellect who would look at me with disdain and
say with the chiding southern drawl, "Surely you don't believe
everything the Bible says is true."

We were each other's witness and we never lost the wonder of that moment, that morning of the Visit. I just know
earth has no words to describe heaven. You will just have to
see it for yourself.

CHAPTER 14

THE GRAND RESCUE

"Lord I can almost see beyond the calamity,
over the mountains.
I know you truly hold the mystery.
I ask one thing —Lord, can I live to see
all my past sins are history?"

– SPENCER MACLEOD '97

1996

The Brockton Juvenile Detention Center was a large non-descript building in the middle of the city. The air inside was greasy and stale, and there was no color, just gray – gray faces, gray food. Spencer hated it. But at his final court date, he turned to me and said, "Why don't I just get this over with?"

We were both tired, cases on top of cases continued over and over while lawyers shrugged and grabbed their briefcases, a morning's wages richer. So the judge gave him 45 days in Brockton, one of many small New England cities, a bleak and busted mill town, about an hour away from the Cape. I watched the bailiff handcuff my son and lead him away, feeling the air get sucked out of me. I was glad I was a half hour from home because I needed all that time to cry, a cry that came up from my gut, a place that mothers come with. By the time I pulled into the driveway, I was done.

"Spence is locked up for 45 days," I told Miles, who was waiting outside. He looked at the driveway, then turned and walked inside, his jaw tense, eyes down.

My friend Sandy and her husband, Steve came over the next day and tried to make me laugh. I got lonely sometimes and felt like a fifth wheel with married people but they were different. They were just ordinary people but they loved my three sons and me and could even make Spence smile when he was trying to act like he was all bad.

She teased me about every new guy in church, but knew I was reluctant to date, let alone remarry. It had been a few years since Tony left, and I intentionally avoided guys, not trusting them or myself. But I didn't want to tell God what I would or wouldn't do, so my only condition was that God would bring him to me and my only request was that this man God found would love Jesus beyond anything else in life. I felt pretty sure those things would only happen in a cheesy Christian movie, so I had forgotten about it – when the phone rang.

"Hi, may I speak with Robin?" a male voice asked.

"Yes, this is Robin." It was a hot August day, and I was feeling impatient.

"Hi, this is C.B. Farnsworth." Pause. "I think we have a few mutual friends, and I've heard about you and wanted to meet you." Pause again.

"I have kids," I said, realizing as it came out of my mouth how rude it sounded.

"I like kids," he said evenly. More silence. Sandy was smiling next to me, listening in.

"Do you like ice cream?" he asked.

"No," I quickly answered, "I don't." I didn't care if I was rude. I was hot and had no time for this.

"How about coffee?"

Persistent. "Yes, I do like coffee," I said, starting to smile and wiping the sweat from my eyes. *Good,* he said, he would bring me some – soon.

After we hung up Sandy looked at me and said, "Aren't you going to shower and change before he comes over?" Heat and humidity have never been kind to my general appearance.

"No. If he doesn't like who I am, then he can leave," I said. Sandy smiled and pulled Steve towards the door.

"Call me!" She waved from outside.

I put a Disney movie on for Jacob, then waited for my coffee outside in the yard. The sun was mercifully sinking into the trees.

A few minutes later, a red pickup truck pulled in and out jumped C.B. Farnsworth, holding two Dunkin' Donuts cups. I introduced him to my flowers and my badly mannered German Shepherd, then settled at the picnic table outside. We talked for two hours, mostly about Jesus, as I drank his coffee with sugar and he drank mine without. Then little Jake opened up the screen door and stepped out onto the porch, focusing on the man sitting across from me.

"Who's that, mom?" The last few months he had been asking me where his father was, even asking random men in the grocery line if they were his dad. I introduced them and C.B. took his cue to leave.

"Can I call you again?" He *was* nice to look at, and I liked that his truck was old and worn.

"Sure," I said, trying to sound casual. I liked him, and I thought I would want to be friends, in a careful way. He liked me too, and told me only much later, after I accepted his proposal, that he knew then he had found the one he was looking for, a sweaty and dirt-streaked version of the Proverbs 31 wife.

Spencer was released in September, after Miles started high school. I picked him up only after an agreement was made; that if he came home, he was under my rules. He was pale and thinner, wearing a dirty white t-shirt; his hair was long and shaggy. Most of his clothes had been stolen. I thought I'd hear about how awful it was, how everyone mistreated him. I was waiting for the rage. He stared out of the window as we crossed the bridge over the Cape Cod Canal.

"I never thought I'd miss the Cape," his voice was soft. "But it's good to be going home."

I noticed small changes at first. The constant arguing was gone. He stayed home a lot, reading. The rap posters came down, the clothes changed. I would find the Bible open on his bed. He spent more time with Miles and Jake, and asked little of me. Something was different, so I kept praying.

New Years Eve. Spence came in and asked if he could go into Boston with some friends. No, I said. He dug in, obstinate, and I could sense the old anger rising. I dug in too.

"C'mon mom!" I stayed on the couch and pretended to read. He turned and with long strides hit the door, letting it bang shut behind him. It was snowing. *Another good reason to say No to Boston,* I thought, but I figured he'd go anyway. The old Spence would've, then paid later. But an hour later, he came through the door, head down, smiling.

"I'm sorry I got mad, mom." I smiled; this was going to be a good new year.

January 1997

Some people get knocked down and God scoops them up. Some people God only has to whisper to get their attention. For Spence, it was as if God had fun pursuing him, showing up on every street corner, behind every tree. In fact, it was a street corner in New York City where the final surrender began; a man with a flyer, shoved in Spencer's hand, then he was gone. It was New York; it could've said anything.

"Expect a miracle," it read. It was from the Times Square Church, a place I had gone to a few times on my own when we had come into the city. He pocketed the tract and went back to my brother's home in Ossining with Miles.

"I can't explain it," he would say later. "I knew it was time. I talked to God before I went to sleep that night after reading that little flyer. In the morning I woke up changed. I was born again."

When he came home from that trip, he looked different. His eyes danced, like when he was a little boy, his jaw relaxed. He laughed from down deep, a gentle rolling laugh. The grueling self-consciousness that had plagued him for years had rolled away. The rage had lifted. God had come up over him like a tidal wave, sudden and fierce in His love, breaking over him, capturing him finally, and when he came up again, the old Spence had washed away. He was free.

One week later we were driving home from church. He had gone down to the altar and made a public commitment to Christ.

"Do you know what mom?" He was riding in the back and I could see his face, softly lit from the flickering streetlights.

"What Spence," I said watching the lights play across his expression.

"I sure do love Jesus." He caught my eyes in the rear view mirror, and then turned to the window. Peace. It occurred to me he had not known any peace in a very long time. That was what I saw on his face.

I left for work that night as he and Miles were lifting weights in the basement. Jake was asleep. Around three in the morning, Spence called me from home.

"Mom, where's the Tylenol? My chest kind of hurts." Okay, he was lifting weights; he pulled something, I said, the nurse in me at attention. I hung up the phone and sat at the nurses' station, unsettled. Something was not right. I called C.B. at his apartment and woke him up.

"Can you go get Spence and bring him to the ER?"

"Sure," he said, half awake. I warned him that Spence would not be thrilled.

The tech pushing Spencer's stretcher from x-ray ran with him to the front. The ER doctor showed me his film – a complete "white-out" of his left lung, meaning the lung was completely deflated. Because of the pressure buildup within his chest he had a tension pneumothorax. His heart was displaced to the right.

"In another hour he would've been in some big trouble," the doctor said, looking at the x-ray on the wall. I felt sick – this was too close. He quickly medicated Spence, then shoved a chest tube into the left side of his chest. Drowsy from sedation, Spence was admitted to the hospital.

The next day, they decided to operate. Because of the total collapse of his lung, they felt he was too high risk for a re-collapse. Post-op, everything that could go wrong, went wrong: vomiting from the pain medicine, a rash from the sheets and he couldn't pee. On the third day after surgery, an artery in his chest somewhere let loose, quickly filling the canister on the floor beside his bed with bright red blood. The surgeon whisked him back to the OR, but by the time he opened him up, it was gone; the bleeding stopped.

Foolish is the Christian who thinks there is no battle ahead, that the path is clear and soft under your feet and led by a choir of angels. Yet this was an immediate and extreme introduction. The journey had begun. Spence was discharged home two weeks later, frail and understanding that many questions sent to heaven are met with silence. Easy to say the battle belongs to the Lord; harder to stand in the midst of it, alone.

CHAPTER 15

A MOTHER'S DISCLAIMER

I had three boys, I have two now. The first one made me a mother. The first one was Spencer, the one I lost. And then for a while, I hated that I had been made a mother, with a heart that could feel so much pain. Any mother who loses a child feels like a failure; it doesn't matter that it makes no sense. And the failure follows like a gray sky that never rains or breaks for the sun – it just oppresses.

Looking back, I was always afraid of losing him, maybe all three. Every mother thinks dark, terrifying thoughts of their child lost, maybe taken, dying alone or found dead, and your heart beats like it's going to break through your chest. Breathing becomes fast and you think you might scream or vomit or pass out, then you gasp for air and you are awake. It's just a dream, but the horror lingers, the day is a shade darker and you think you should love your kids more or maybe less until you forget the dream and it's all back to normal.

But the truth is, there was something always unsure about Spencer, the first boy. Maybe it was his lack of fear, like the time I found him hanging on the end of a small branch about 80 feet over a rushing river in Maine, laughing. He was five. Or the policeman who brought the seven-year-old boy home after spotting his bright blue sweatshirt swaying back and forth at the top of a sixty-foot pine tree down the road. And a few feet below was a red sweatshirt – Miles, following his big brother.

Then the teen years, the fearlessness mixed with rage and a mouth that did not know how to *Shhhhhh* made him more frightening. Black eyes and a busted nose did not subdue him, not a bit.

He punched holes in my walls, punched others but never threatened me or even swore although one time I was so mad at him I flipped over a table and broke a leg off, holding it up like a baseball bat. I must've looked crazy because he jumped out of the window, just turned and jumped, two stories up and I ran to the window in time to watch him run across the yard, jump a split rail fence and disappear into the darkness. I knew he was smiling too.

But there were times of peace, like a wide-open meadow stuffed with flowers and chirping birds. Short times, but enough to plant a seed of hope in a mother's heart.

I never wanted a daughter. I was mostly afraid of recreating myself, then becoming my own mother. So God gave me three sons.

Spence was a lot of me wrapped up in a boy. I saw it emerge slowly over the years – the Fearless, the Fighter, then the Rebel. When we fought, we were two rams, heads down, horns smashing and cracking like canons. But when he quit school, I understood. When he fell in love with hazelnut coffee and military history and every kind of music, I saw my

DNA dressed in a hoodie. Then, when God came up over him, the Lord of hosts, riding the heavenly armies in a great cloud of glory and Spence said, *I surrender, you got me*, I said *That's my boy.*

In the spring of '97 Spencer entered the Brockton Teen Challenge, a Christian addiction ministry birthed in the 1950's by David Wilkerson. Spence was not addicted to drugs or alcohol at the time, although he had done it all at some point and it was a screaming temptation. He knew he was weak – spiritually and emotionally; and he was lonely. Our church was sparse with young people.

Teen Challenge meant a year commitment, so the decision was wrestled through prayerfully. Home was a good place then. Miles was excelling in school and basketball and Spence was his friend and mentor. I was dating C.B. and little Jacob was serving as our joyful chaperone. But Spencer was keenly aware of his frailty and he knew that there was a lot at stake if he fell away.

It was a good move. Although at age 17 he was the youngest person there, he thrived in an atmosphere of discipline and redemption. He was able to find the time to write – rap in particular, and to read. The day began with prayer, then Bible class for three hours. They also helped him earn his GED.

For his dad and me, they were the best of days, because our son had been rescued. I knew the power of Jesus Christ to save and to set free; I knew it for myself and had seen this same miracle over and over again through the years in every kind of person and circumstances imaginable. But to witness the change in Spence was jaw dropping. He pursued God with a rare intensity, a focus so passionate that at times I secretly worried. How can you maintain that? At the same time, it was convicting, in the purest sense. To be with Spence, for everyone, felt like standing next to Jesus.

But also the closer he drew to the holiness of God, the more aware he became of his own shortcomings. The light magnifies the fault-lines; pride, selfishness, fear. This is where only the grace and mercy of God can keep us moving forward. And this is where Spencer fell short; receiving that gift for himself.

C.B. and I married October 11th of that year. A week earlier, Jacob had turned his little round face with the big glasses up to C.B. and asked, "Can I start calling you dad *now*?"

It was a joyous, crazy event. Although it was my third wedding, it felt like the first. I even had my hair done and wore a long soft blush gown – a first in my lifetime, and I'm sure the last. I walked down the aisle with Spence and Miles on either side of me, little Jacob in his new Sears suit with our rings in his pocket out front. I was leaving my sweet church that had been a safe refuge for five years, and entering into a new church family – C.B.'s church, a large, boisterous group with a love for Jesus and lots of teens.

There were songs and testimonies – a blend of our two churches celebrating our union. But the highlight was Spencer. He wrote a rap the night before called "Match Made in Heaven" (he spelled it "Mach"; he was a horrific speller), a soft, ballad-type of rap that had strings in the background. I didn't know rap could be tender.

"Mach Made in Heaven"

by Spencer Macleod Oct. 10 1997
  (Spelling corrected)

  Now as we dwell together
  As sisters and brethren
  To see a match made in heaven
  We realize that it's a blessing
  But there's another side of the story
  That's hidden – and as I speak
  You should see how God has His hand
  In this since the beginning

Spencer's lyrics traced our family history: two divorces, crazy teenagers, and our exodus to salvation.

  Now through all the insanity
  You knew that God would provide for our family
  You and Jesus – all else is vanity
  Conquering trials while
  Planting seeds in your child
  And through your worst heartache you kept a smile
  All the worthwhile
  You kept your eyes to the sky
  I remember seeing you cry

Then he recounted his own turning away from God…

  You had three sons
  But one was running
  But Jesus brought him in

Then He gave you a husband

I know you love him
A real man
And by your side he'll stand
It's a beautiful plan
Together walkin' hand in hand
At the altar exchanging wedding bands
I know you both understand
Can't nobody love you like Jesus can

I was captivated in my seat, watching my beautiful son with a mike in his hand, shy but sure. The final verse and chorus before the church erupted in cheers...

C.B. and Robin's weddin'
Saturday October 11
We give our mother away
Just wanna say
We'll remember you when
we pray
You're moving on to a brighter day

Chorus:
Wedding bells are ringing
Angels up above are singing
God's children havin' a weddin'
It's a match made in heaven .

Lives are being changed
And vows are being exchanged
People coming together to see a
Match made in heaven

Saturday October 11
C.B. and Robin's weddin'...
A match made in heaven

C.B. and I kissed for the first time at the altar and after a simple reception in the lobby, I washed all of the hairspray out of my hair, and off we went in his pickup truck, towing a pop up camper someone lent us. It was fall, just chilly enough to draw us very close together. The trees were on fire as we headed north through the Berkshires, and we imagined God turned it up just for us. A Mach made in heaven.

CHAPTER 16

SOUL ON FIRE

*"The fear of not doing any thing should be
greater than the fear of doing it."*

– SPENCER'S JOURNAL, '98

*When we put pride to death, God imparts power and implants
hope. We rise renewed. But when we revert to our self-sufficient
ways, the Spirit presses in. And so we must return to the cross,
mortifying the martyr in us, destroying the self-display. As we
hold fast to the cross, God offers the spirit of humility.
Stray from the cross and humility recedes, pride returns.
It is simple. It's the cross. Again I say, the cross.
I didn't say it was easy, just simple.*

– ROY HESSION, "THE CALVARY ROAD"
(FOUND COPIED AND TAPED ON A DRESSER
NEXT TO SPENCER'S PILLOW)

Saturday morning. Out of work by 0730 then home. No sleep today. Jacob and Miles are still asleep. I peel off my scrubs and shower, considering a 10-minute nap for fuel. I pass out on the couch and awaken to Jake's shout from the stairs.

"Mama?" Little feet peddling down the stairs. In the winter we fight over whose turn it is to sleep with Jacob, because his body is a small but efficient furnace, and when he's out, he won't move much, not like Spence and Miles who would pummel me from both sides when they were little, a tangle of knees and elbows.

Saturday mornings are Brockton trips. Jake will always be with me, and usually Miles, if I can rouse him from bed.

When we pull into the long driveway behind the big white house on Main St. you can almost sense you are on holy ground, like Jesus is there celebrating. Time and motion take on a different dimension. Young men stroll across the campus, calling out to each other. Some are with visiting wives or parents; there is easy laughter like everyone is saying, "Whew, that was close!" Singing comes from the kitchen.

"Spencer's mom!" A tall black man with a wide toothy smile waves his long arm towards me. "He's in his room!" he calls out to us, motioning to a more modern brick building in the back. As we change direction, Spence rounds the corner, grinning, notebook in hand, navy jacket on over a plaid shirt that is tucked into khaki pants. His clothes are mostly donated, his sneakers are from K-Mart. I smile thinking about how he would've reacted to K-Mart shoes a year ago.

We head towards the gym, a large room used for everything from basketball to banquets. It smells more like a gym than anything else but you can catch the smell of bacon coming through the door. Bacon and sweat – a guy paradise. The singing in the kitchen is louder.

"Nothing but the blood of Jesus..." The voice lifts through the air, a stream of pure praise calling down heaven.

"That's Morris," Spence nods with a smile. "He can cook *and* sing!"

After the boys shoot around in the gym, we climb in the car. Spence is learning how to drive so I take my seat beside him. Even though he used to steal my car when he was 14, he didn't know how to drive then. I remember one night a cop came to my door, waking me up around two.

"Sorry to disturb you, ma'am, but your neighbors called. They saw someone pull your car into your driveway with the lights off and sure enough I felt the hood and it's warm."

Spence had come up quietly behind me, wearing his boxers, listening silently.

"I see." I see I'm not an idiot, but I was too tired to address it then. "Thanks, officer." He looked like a rookie.

"I'm glad everything's okay," I offered.

He hesitated, looked at the car, then back to me, with Spence looming behind me. "Yes, ma'am. Sorry to bother you." And he was gone.

The next day I was driving Spence and his friend Jermaine across town. I popped a cassette in.

"I like your new cassette deck mom," Spence had said, sitting beside me.

"Oh yeah? Good! " I checked the rear view mirror and saw Jermaine's dark eyes averting my gaze.

"I bought it so you guys could enjoy your music when you steal my car while I'm asleep." I heard Spence make a little choking sound and I got to see Jermaine's eyes almost drop out of his head. That was worth it all.

After driving around Brockton, we pull into the Brockton Mall, which is a bunch of dollar stores strung together and we grab lunch at a Burger King. Spence sets Jake on his lap and asks him how he's doing and plays with his cheeks, which are hard to resist, big soft pillows beneath his glasses. On the ride back to Teen Challenge I drive and Spence takes out his notebook. He's written down questions – from sermons, from dreams, from songs. And they are good questions; ones that make you stop and realize that there is more, much more to God's kingdom than the answers you have stored.

I have a dull night-shift hangover, but there is such a beautiful peace in that old Chevy Celebrity sedan as we roll down Main St., Spence with his notebook open, his eyes bright and child-like, Miles, respectfully in awe of his big brother, and Jacob, happy just to be a part of this family, and the wondrous expectation we all sense although none of us could name it.

There is a picture Spence took from his room at Teen Challenge looking west, across the parking lots, the gym with the large **Teen Challenge** sign over the doorway. Offices were attached, but now darkened, and behind the winter trees, you could see the poverty of the neighbors, the multifamily goliaths that stood close together, allowing just a little sky in between. But what you saw was not Teen Challenge or its neighbors. Your gaze was brought upward, to a ray of light breaking over an enormous cloud, streaking it with swaths of gold and deep orange – then the sky beneath falling behind the darkened world in majestic purple and cobalt. The trees lifted black fingers into the sky, as if in praise. I can see him now with the camera, looking up, homeward.

"Robin, it's for you." A nurse at the station put the call on hold. It's around three in the morning. Who would call?

"Hello?"

"Mom..."

"Hey Spence!" I knew something was wrong. I waited.

"Mom, I can't do this. There's things in me that God can't change. I'm too stubborn...too full of pride." The voice was a little above a whisper and sounded tortured.

"Spence, honey, we all feel that way, that there's things in us that God can't change. But there's grace! Just keep pressing forward."

"I can't!" He raised his voice slightly, then sighed. I knew he was tired.

"Why are you up so late? Isn't there a curfew?"

"I was just reading my Bible. I came to the part about Saul. I'm Saul, mom. I think God's mad at me."

"You're not Saul!" My voice was rising now, and I looked around, realizing how strange this conversation might sound to my co-workers.

"You're not Saul," I repeated, calmer. This was not the first time I had to talk Spence down. It seemed these attacks of condemnation always followed a time of victory, of joy. He had been writing rap and traveling with the choir, sharing his testimony. He was also making plans to come home. Stupid devil. We bantered back and forth for twenty minutes, then I told him I would come up after work. It was a Tuesday, I would be really tired, but I hated hearing the torment in his voice.

When I got there, Charles, the dean, met me.

"Hey, Spencer's upstairs in the office." I shuddered, remembering many trips to the principal's office on Spencer's behalf in middle and high school. I followed Charles up the steps. The director, the assistant director and Spencer sat in comfortable chairs in a large paneled office.

Jim, the director smiled and stood when he saw me.

"Come in, come in… have a seat." Spence looked up at me and gave a half smile. I was relieved.

"So, we've all been sharing notes and talking to Spencer. We have some concerns, and we're glad you're here," Jim began. The other men were quiet, letting Jim speak for them.

"It seems that Spence has been fasting almost all of his meals." The other two guys nodded. "No one knew until we started to watch and compare notes. And he's lost some weight."

Yes, I saw that too. For a boy that loved to eat, he had a little to lose; maybe 15 to 20 pounds.

"And, his roommates claim he stays up every night to two or three in the morning," Jim said, leaning forward in his chair, causing Charles and the other guy to scoot forward too.

"Doing what?" I felt I had to ask.

"Praying," Charles spoke now. "They say he's on his knees, praying and reading the Bible. Sometimes for hours and it makes it hard for them to sleep."

I looked at Spence, who was looking at the floor.

"Don't get me wrong!" Jim interjected. "We love Spencer's passion for the Lord. But we have concerns." I did too, and I did not want to mention the phone call, although I had a hunch they knew that side of Spencer, the tormented side. It had been there since the beginning: the collapsed lung. He wondered if God was angry with him. He never felt like he could do enough, was good enough. There were small pockets of peace and rest, then the battle raged on.

Spencer agreed to eat and not to stay up so late praying. He walked me to my car. We were both tired. I opened my arms and he stooped down to hug me. Eighteen years old. I remembered telling my pastor about his zeal and love for Jesus.

"He probably has a great call on his life," he said, and then added, "If he makes it."

Jesus, I need to see you. Help me to run after you, to yell, "Hey Jesus! Over here!" Is that bad? Thank you for your easy yoke. No fronts, no fears. Nothing to hide, nothing to prove. Nothing to lose. Thank you. Amen.

– SPENCER'S JOURNAL, FEBRUARY 24ᵀᴴ 1999

The thing about Spence is how much you never knew until he was gone. Still, if you watched closely, which a mother does when no one is looking, you saw peculiar things – things that sometimes irritated me, because I knew how his mind overworked, how high he held the bar for himself. The other kids in church saw it too. Some made fun of him, some felt like I inevitably did – convicted of my spiritual laziness and inspired to do more.

He sought out all of his old friends when he got home from Teen Challenge and told them of how Jesus had changed him and that Jesus loved them too. Most said, *That's good for you, Spence, but not for me.* A few came to church sporadically but didn't stick. Still Spencer prayed, keeping lists, names that would pop up on his calendar next to "oil change." *Pray for Jermaine, Tim F., Liz, Pastor Campo, Alex.* "Buy a car" next to *Jackie, Miles, Richie, Dad, Adam.*

Prayer was the language of his heart.

God help me to_know_ and to live like the time is short.
Tomorrow is really _not_ promised. To give you all today.

– SPENCER, '99

The image sits in my memory like a peculiar piece of a puzzle that I can't find a place for. It could be missed; it was missed the first several times I watched the footage from South Africa, when 40 members of our church landed there in March of 2000. I can instantly smell the red dirt, the pungent sweat, and the pots of liquid stew in the small shacks that looked like dirty water.

Then the crowds, mostly teens, in schools from Johannesburg to Port Elizabeth, their uniforms bright and crisp. They had exotic names like Zulu, Xhosa. They were black as coal, and I see Spence standing among them, tanned from the scorching sun. His face is relaxed, focused.

"He was in his element there," someone told me recently. He made friends, preferring them to his peers that traveled with us. In Port Elizabeth, he befriended a small group of street orphans and took them to the hotel where he and others clothed and fed them. In the early morning, with the sound of the birds waking I would hear, "Spensuh!" in a loud whisper coming up from the street. There they were, four ragged little boys with big clothes on. "Spen-suh!!"

The footage skips from concerts where Spence is onstage rapping with others from the church, inside schools, to the streets; impromptu concerts in a marketplace, walking down the dirt paths of Soweto and Port Elizabeth. You see us all laughing, taking pictures, mostly detached from the hopelessness of a small country ravaged with AIDS, from homeless kids, their hair orange from malnutrition, from the dust just settling in the dried blood of apartheid.

Stop – right there. Behind the group of us lingering near the stage, snapping pictures of the sea of uniformed high school students, in the back, I see Spence, eyes closed, hands lifted to heaven, lips moving. He is alone, against a wall in the shadows – his expression a little sad but at peace.

When we returned to America with our suitcases stuffed with cheap suits and salad spoons, I noticed Spencer's was empty. Only a mother notices these things, only I saw that he had given away almost everything, even his Bible. The only thing he bought was a book about Soweto. A card was tucked in the middle of the book – a disturbing photograph of a black man running with his dead child in his arms, still bleeding from bullet holes in his limp little body. The man was crying.

Our pastor asked everyone who went on the trip to stand up and share what the trip meant to them after we returned. Most everyone talked about the poverty, of how grateful we were for what we had. Some of us thought we would return as missionaries some day, but we never did.

"I don't think I'll ever go back," Spencer said when it was his turn. "But I get to see all my friends in heaven some day."

Like I said, there's some things that only a mother picks up. Some things made me so scared. *Why are you talking about heaven?* Yet with the fear always came a rush of awe and wonder. His face, eyes closed, hands lifted, in pure worship. That's the same image I see when I picture my son now, as I write this. Only his face is slightly turned away from me. He is facing the glory of God's throne. And I don't have to see it to know. Joy. *Joy unspeakable and full of glory.*

CHAPTER 17

LAST YEAR ON EARTH

May 25 1999

More than anything I need a heavenly perspective of this world. If I won't get desperate, I won't get anywhere. Desperation is one of the main ingredients to faith. Desperation is a condition, but our choice is: Will we acknowledge our condition and position and acknowledge our only hope out of that condition, Jesus Christ? The devil's deadline and plan or God's plan? Lot or Abraham? Heaven or Here and Now? God, please help me to see my desperation and Your hope. Other lives and mine are at stake. Please let me know Satan's strategy.

– SPENCER'S JOURNAL

May 2001

There wasn't much to look at – just a slight rise in the earth next to what looked like a trench around it. Neatly mowed grass covered it all, including the infamous Crater, another Civil War battle site not far from this one. Spence walked along the grassy ridge, looking out into the woods that sprang up suddenly, about fifty feet away.

It was a clear May afternoon, and you would sooner expect to see golfers than soldiers. Keeping his eyes into the woods, he walked down the sloping hill, stopping about 20 feet from the thick forest. I came along side of him to see what had captured his interest. We stood staring ahead, silent except for the soft clatter of wildlife deep in the woods.

"They were so close," he said finally.

It took a few seconds for me to get it. The soldiers. I looked at the woods some more, straining to see what he saw there.

"I mean, they could see each other, their faces. They had to get so close." Suddenly the woods came alive with smoke and the stench of gunpowder, the deafening crack of the musket, shells ripping through the trees, taking wood, flesh, bone.

The small mound behind us was called a fort. It wasn't much more than a bunch of cut down trees fortifying a dirt hill. I looked at the clipped grass. Blood, blood covered this ground before the grass did. Most of these soldiers were boys belonging to families, telling their mamas they would be home again. I turned and watched Jake running along the ridge. He was not terribly impressed with this fort.

We were on our way to Edisto for a week, and to pick up Miles at college in Charleston. Spence worked for a guy in church as a carpenter, and seemed to have found something he liked and was good at. He got the week off and we headed out in Spencer's Ford Explorer. I hoped this trip would help him get perspective. He had not been doing well.

That winter he had pulled himself out of all ministry, saying he wasn't worthy to serve in a public forum. He struggled with the same thing all young guys struggled with –girls, thoughts of girls. Purity was essential to him and he felt

incompetent. Compounded with his fruitless labors evange-
lizing old friends, he sunk into deep despair.

As we stood side by side at the edge of the woods in
Virginia, I wondered where his mind was going. It was like
when he got injured playing soccer in middle school and I
jumped from the bleachers, Super-Mom flying to the rescue,
but then he looked up from the ground and his glare caught
me in mid-air, saying, *Don't you dare!* And I stopped, and stood
foolish and helpless from the sidelines as the coach attended to
my son. Now again, I had to watch him walk away, remembering that he was God's now – the same boy who climbed
too high, who swam too far. He was searching and I wanted to
find it for him but I couldn't.

We rented a cottage across the street from the ocean I
called the Ugly House with fake blue paneling, lots of vinyl
and nautical knick knacks from a dollar store. You didn't
expect or want high end living on Edisto, but this house was
so ugly it was funny.

In the morning, a mockingbird belted out its repertoire
for me, the ocean breeze teased through the screen, bringing
salt and memories of waking up to the waves as a young girl.
Back then, metal cots were pulled out onto the big screen
porch overlooking the ocean and my brothers would be close
by. In the morning with the sun at the edge of the ocean, we
would rise like a tribe of sea dogs, dreams of pirates or lonely
ghosts wiped from our eyes, to a day of fishing or just looking
for more shells. That was all and it was enough. Simple times.

I cooked piles of eggs and grits and shrimp because that's
the easiest way to say *I love you* to sons. Spence was 21, Miles
19 and Jake just 9, elated to be with both big brothers, a basketball and an ocean of waves.

But the cloud over Spencer would not break. I don't think Miles could see it, although he was used to his brother's quirky side, the places that were too deep to follow. But I did; the line of his brow, the eyes restless and sad. He was quiet, withdrawn and raw like an open wound. I spoke carefully.

"Spence, can't you just enjoy your salvation like other kids?"

"I'm not even sure I'm saved, Mom." We were on the beach and he turned to face the open sky, but his voice cracked just a bit, and I knew he wanted to cry but he was a man now. The waves rolled up the sand, reaching towards us.

"That's crazy Spencer! God does not give up on us, no matter how many times we fall. He loves you!"

He would not face me. His head dropped then looked up again. He turned and sighed, looking down the beach. Only a few people walked along, heads down looking for shells and sharks teeth.

"I think He must be getting pretty tired of me. I know I am."

"He doesn't get tired Spence. Never." I tried to get his eyes to meet mine. He looked at me and gave a quick smile, then turned to leave.

"I'll see you at the Ugly House," he said. I got him to smile, I thought. That's good.

"The free gift of grace with which God perfects our efforts may come in many ways, but I am convinced that it is the common experience of Christians that it does come. There may be some souls, whose brave and bitter lot it is to conquer comfortless.

Soft moments of peace with God and man may never come to
him. He may feel himself viler than a thousand trumpery souls
who could not have borne his trials for a day. For you and me
is reserved no such cross and no such crown as theirs who falling
still fight, and fighting fall, with their faces Zionwards, into the
arms of the everlasting Father. 'As one whom his mother comfor-
teth' (Isaiah 61) shall be the healing of their wounds."

– JULIANA HORATIA EWING

Spence had it in his head that he was a man now, and
men should be on their own. He could not convince the other
guys in church of this, who preferred the free rent of their parents' basements. So he left. I was alarmed at first, but because
he worked for a man in church, steadily, I felt I had eyes on
behind the scenes. Over the summer, Spence sat in the back of
the church, and then he was gone.

"I can't stand people looking at me and thinking I'm a
good Christian; I'm not."

Our pastor was a big Italian guy from Queens, New York,
with fire in his eyes. He loved to laugh and hated pretense.
He counseled Spencer closely, trying to show him that he suffered from nothing uncommon, steering him towards God's
redemption and grace, and perhaps he should just date a nice
girl in the church. But Spence had his mind set.

"I'm not broken enough. I'm too prideful," he'd say, like
he was pronouncing a sentence. So he set out to find the end
of himself.

Reports came back, disconcerting; he was found sleeping
in his car, a mother of one of his old friends that I worked
with told me she was surprised to see Spencer coming around
so much.

"Don't worry," she told me. "He only drinks Coke. They all know he's different now."

But something churned within me. Her sons were young men now like mine, but inside I felt fear and hostility towards them, the same ones my son had prayed for. They were lovable at a distance, now everything was too close and the mother bear in me was up on her hind legs. I sensed trouble.

In the fall, he decided to move in with a couple that just returned from pastoring in Chicago. Because he was living with and working for people in my church, I felt better. There were people watching him.

"Mom. What is going on with Spence?" Miles asked. There was no quick answer.

"I don't know. Just pray."

He stayed connected to a few friends in church, but it was a strained connection. He was there, but distant. Pastor Campo would call him up and meet him for lunch.

Your boy is doing fine. He's coming back, he would tell me, knowing that I worried, but by the next day, Spence would be confused again, entangled in voices that kept him away.

"I make a terrible backslider, Ma," he told me one day when he stopped by. "I drive around in my car, listening to preaching tapes. I park at the beach and read my Bible."

His voice trailed off. He seemed tired but restless, like a soul caught between two worlds, haunted and haunting.

The Dream

Carl and Spence settled into the booth at Joe's Diner, taking their time from the cold December day. The coffee was hot and Carl held the fat mug in his hands, savoring the warmth, the smell. Spence stared at his plate, pushing the food around. Usually Spence was far ahead of him when it came to eating. They had been working together for months now, and you get to know someone, their habits. Was he sick?

"What's up with you, man?"

Spence gently rested his fork in his eggs.

"I had the weirdest dream last night."

"Yeah?"

Spence looked up quickly at Carl, then away, at the tables filled with working guys like them.

"I was at my church. It was a funeral, I guess." The waitress came by with a coffee pot, and Carl held out his cup, but Spence didn't see her.

"There was a casket up front, and I asked Pastor Campo, 'Whose funeral is it?' And he looked at me and he said, 'It's your funeral, Spence.'"

Spencer looked at Carl, who took a sip of his coffee, and looked down, unsure of what to say. This was too weird, man. We better get back to work.

January 2002

"He shall preserve thy soul..." If you can believe that, you're all set. They may kill you but "nothing can separate you from the love (how much do I have to learn about the <u>true</u> meaning of this word) of Christ."

– SPENCER'S JOURNAL

When I think of the winter leading into 2002, I get immensely sad, overtaken with an urge to rescue, to grab my son and run and run and run. He seemed pressed, boxed in to a corner and I wondered where was a place for him.

"At first we were glad to see Spence back," his friend Jay told me. "But he was clearly not the same. We almost felt like we had to watch over him."

My mind would flip through the file of usual places – he could return to Teen Challenge, to church, back home, out of state to relatives. I had been through this weighing of options so many times during his teen years. But it was different now. He was a man, very capable. Yet there was something hidden and fragile within him. I felt like I was losing him.

New Years Day we went to the house where he lived for a small gathering, mostly older couples. We drank soda and played Pictionary. Even for me, it was boring and I was aware of Spence in the periphery, trying to politely belong. I broke away to see how he was, looking for an opening, a crack in the wall I could slip through.

"Spence, why don't you show your mom your room?" someone asked.

He looked relieved that he could leave the party. I followed him down the basement stairs. As we turned right into his room, I was struck by one thought – *it looks like no one lives here.* The bed was neatly made, the walls stark and white, not a picture, a poster. When he lived at home, the walls told you who he was; the angry teen put up surly rap stars, athletes with attitude. Then the redeemed and saved Spence replaced Tupac with a huge poster inscribed with the names of Christ, *I AM* in bold centered in the middle. Pictures of family went up.

A bare light bulb hung too low in the middle of the room, giving it an aseptic look. A brand new coffee maker with stickers still on it sat on his table. Several other Christmas presents I recognized lay untouched next to it. I used my mother scanning system to detect any sign of what direction his life was heading in, but that was the thing. There seemed to be no life. Everything he was he carried within, locked behind the dark blue eyes, the eyes looking for God.

"I like your room," I lied.

"Thanks mom." He looked at me, then away. I could hear laughter, heavy steps above. I felt scared. *Jesus, help me.*

I hate to fast. I know, I know it's important, it's in the Bible. Jesus did it, a lot. But still I get surly and petulant and as the hunger pangs begin ringing out my intestines, I get mad at Jesus. This seems counter-productive. But I felt a great sense of urgency deep within my spirit that January. There was an unpredictability that had attached itself to this boy since he was a baby. He rolled off a bed when he wasn't supposed to roll. He stood up and said, *Mushroom*, instead of Mama or Dada before he was one. He climbed, swung, jumped in death-defying leaps, but snapped his arm by simply dropping two feet to the soft grass from a jungle gym at a neighbor's house. Later on came the fights, the phone calls: *We have your son down here at the police station.*

Then he met Jesus, and the rage was gone, in a moment, so gone, he looked different. His face relaxed, the tense jaw now prone to an easy smile, the eyes that defied and dodged truth turned playful and inquisitive, even shy.

Yet the lack of fear stayed. Why would God remove this boldness that he so delighted in? The young man that would witness to a doctor about Jesus healing, to a thug on the streets of the Bronx about God's love, to a cop at a basketball game about salvation. But now it scared me. What next?

I was reading Jon Krakauer's *Into the Wilderness,* a true story of a young man who just drove off to nowhere one day, a bright, beautiful man only to be finally found dead in Alaska, from eating poisonous berries. But the tragedy wasn't the berries; it was his inability to fit in, so he just kept running. I grabbed the book and hid it when Spence came over one day to pick up Jake for a basketball game. I could tell he was wearing out. He loved to read and I didn't want him to get any ideas.

I picked a day in January to fast and to really pray. I stayed inside, circling the house, tempted with distractions but sharply aware of the fear inside, like a black water swamp rising. Did I just mess this kid up so bad that he couldn't be fixed? I could feel the sticky breath of Darkness, the Accuser. *He's mine, He's mine, He's mine.*

I dropped to my knees in the living room, burying my face in an old stuffed chair. *Please God; don't let the devil steal his testimony,* I yelled into the pillow. I was then aware of my own exhaustion, how fear can make you a slave. I knelt there silently for what seemed a long time, then felt a beautiful peace come up on me.

No, he's mine, I heard God speak. *I've got him. He's mine.*

Thank you, Jesus, I whispered into the pillow. More peace, lovely and sweet. It had been a while. Then I felt excited. I could look up again. Spence was going to be all right.

There was one other thing God impressed upon my heart then; that I should ask Spencer for his forgiveness – for times that haunted me, when a four year old boy needed a normal home, arms around him, a mom who was happy and not angry and hung-over, a mom and a dad who loved each other instead of acting like two 13 year olds at a school dance, giving their rings back.

But this request didn't make sense because Spence and I had already been down this road; at Teen Challenge, he had asked some hard questions and I gave him the truth. I apologized and he forgave.

Tell him you're sorry. When God speaks to you, He makes sure you hear.

Okay, I will.

The beef stew was simmering on the stove when I heard the kitchen door open and close, then the familiar steps, shhh-lump, shhh-lump. *He drags his feet like his mother,* I had often thought. It's a subconscious slide of the heel, and then the classic forward bent posture, passed down through my genes, as if our head is in a bigger rush than the rest of our body.

"Hey Spence!" I called out, making my way to the kitchen.

"Hey Ma." He was in his work clothes, layers of clothes; work boots, sweater, Carhartt vest. I could smell sawdust and a hint of sweat. He looked at me, then the stove, smiling. He and Jake had gone to Boston, to watch the Celtics the night before, Spencer's Christmas gift to his littlest brother and I had asked him to come back for dinner tonight.

Miles had returned to college the week before and had just called with the news that he had broken his wrist, putting him on the bench for the rest of the basketball season.

"How did he do that?" Spence asked, taking off his vest.

"He punched a wall during practice," I said matter-of-factly. This was not a new behavior for my son with the quick temper. Spence smiled, and shook his head. The walls in both of their bedrooms were peppered with small dents and holes.

Jake swung through the kitchen, looking at the stew, his brother.

"Hey Jake, what's up?"

"What's up," Jake said, the little brother, not so little at age nine, all feet and legs. They recapped some of the night before, guy-talk I was used to, noting how Jake's voice changed into a Big Guy around Spence. *Adorable.* A mother would never say that out loud. I thought I should check the stew.

Looked good, as I stirred it in the big pot. Perfect for a cold January night. Spence came over and stood next to me, leaning against the counter.

"Looks good, Ma."

"So what's going on?" I had not forgotten, I could not forget, what God had asked of me. The conversation was light and hopeful. Spence was planning on finding a new place with a couple of guys from church. And he wanted to call the pastor and talk.

"He'd love to hear from you, Spence." I knew that was true. Pastor Campo always asked how he was, even asked if there was something he could get him for Christmas.

"I don't know about that." We both stared at the steam rising off of the stew. *Now? This is weird. Okay, now.*

"Spence, there's something I want to say, that God wants me to say to you."

He folded his arms, and I could feel his eyes on my face.

"Okay, shoot."

"You know, I haven't always been a good mom to you." I paused, feeling for direction. Spence shifted his weight, turning more towards me. I kept stirring, even though the stew was fine without me.

"In fact, I was a lousy mom when you were such a little guy, but old enough to really need me there. And I wasn't."

"Mom," he started.

"No I have to say this. I just want you to know I'm so sorry Spence." I looked up at him and noticed he was not sad or mad. What I saw was compassion.

"Mom, you have been the best mom in the whole world." I did not want to cry so I kept stirring that stew.

"Look, I'm a man now. And I take full responsibility for who I am, for the decisions I make. I hate that victim mentality."

"Okay." I looked up at him, his head bent, waiting for me, smiling. I smiled too.

"Let's eat!"

We held hands while Spence prayed over the food. *His hands are rough now. Man's hands,* I remember thinking. Hands that gripped a hammer all week, built houses instead of forts in the woods. The peace that had flooded my living room the day I had fasted and prayed drifted through the kitchen now. *Yes, God has a hold of him, my boy, this beautiful man.*

I did not realize until much later that God had me say all that for me, not for Spence. I would not see him alive again.

Me and my brothers shortly before Tim's death. Left to rt. Tim, Bob (behind), Graham and me.

Spencer at three months

Spencer and Miles, Edisto Island 1984

Alaska 1984

Spencer and Miles with Triple Play 1991

1996, before Jesus

1997, after Jesus, Teen Challenge banquet

1998, in favorite t-shirt, Ephesians 6:12

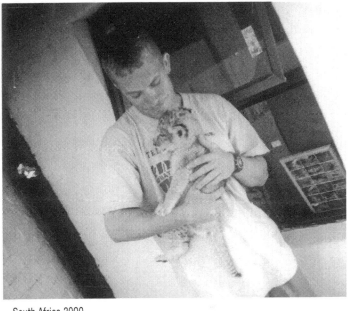

South Africa 2000

Street concert and testimony

High school outreach, Port Elizabeth

With new South African friends

Jake, Miles, Spencer Edisto, 2001.

From left, Brandon Gomes, Julio Jermaine Concepcion (holding a photo of Spencer MacLeod) and Dave Murphy say they've changed their lives following the death of MacLeod.

Murder jolts three into changing lives

Cape Cod Times, 2004

PART TWO

*In my dream I see Jesus running. The dream is in slow motion,
so I can see his stride is long, almost flying, a long robe swirled
around him. He has a look of fierce concentration on His face,
but it is also soft, because of course He knows. He is running to
catch a little girl who is falling, falling like dropped from the sky.
And the girl is me.*

Awake...

1.

THE SHADOW OF DEATH

"My idea of God is not a divine idea. It has to be shattered time after time. He shatters it Himself."

– C.S. LEWIS, *A GRIEF OBSERVED*

January 26th, 2002

We came through the door from the hospital, and Jake stumbled down the hall, back to bed.

Yes, he should be tired. C.B. woke him at 3:30. I wanted him there, with me in the ER. Miles, Miles, I have to call Miles.

I sat at the table and picked up the phone. It was six in the morning on a Saturday. No college student is awake. I let the phone ring and ring, each time pleading for someone to pick up when the answering machine clicked on. Finally I called the local police, who called the campus security.

"Tell him to call his mother," I told him. I sat next to the phone, rocking back and forth, waiting, rocking.

Miles, I said when he called. *Miles, Spencer's dead. He's been killed.*

I heard a thump as the phone dropped then a cry. *No, no, no...*

I'm so sorry, Miles. I'm so sorry, I said into the phone again and again, my son wailing in the distance. A man's voice then...

"Ma'am?"

Yes. The voice was gentle, breaking.

"Ma'am, I'm with security. I want you to know I will stay here with your boy until someone can come to stay with him."

Thank you, I whispered.

Next my brother Graham. We had planned a trip to New York, to Uncle Graham's in just three weeks, to celebrate Spencer's 22nd birthday.

Graham, Spencer's dead. I hear his wife sobbing next to him, his voice crumbling.

Graham, go get Miles. Bring him home.

I stand, not knowing why, and look around. My eyes catch my Bible on top of the radio, the radio Spence and Miles gave me last Christmas. I pick it up and open it.

Maybe God is here, somewhere in here, and I let it fall open, the words swirling before me on the page. Psalm 1:3. My eyes focus.

And he shall be like a tree planted by the rivers of water that bringeth forth his fruit in his season.

I close the cover and put the book down softly. That was before...

I walk into the living room and stop by the window. The sky was cloudless, cobalt. I could hear helicopters. State troopers, looking for my son's killers, my husband would inform me.

You must forgive, the Voice spoke.

There You are now, I said inside. *I thought maybe You were gone, You were mad at me...*

Will you forgive?

I thought of the young men I did not even know yet, no names to attach to the hands with my son's blood upon them. Running, running. The cop in the ER, the tall, thin one with kind eyes.

"Your son was a hero, he saved someone's life." I could only lock onto his eyes, like I was trying to stay afloat. I couldn't speak. "We will make arrests by the end of the day. You have my word." The funny half-bow, then walked away.

I stared at the sky. It's just another day. In New York, my mother falls into my older brother's arms, pounding his chest with her small clenched fists. *No, no, no...*

Yes, I said, still looking up. *I will forgive.*

I looked around the silent room. *People are coming. I should clean the bathroom.* I turned from the sky and walked out of the room.

I told Pastor Campo in the ER to ask everyone at church to leave me alone. It was an odd request that explained itself more in time. I had no strength to deflect or carry words that would add to the weight of this pain. I grew up hearing from my mother the stupid things people said when someone died, but why did I fear my church family the most? So as the traffic picked up through the house, it became a swirling mix of neighbors, my sons' friends, family and an odd array of folks that dropped by to just to hug me, which in hindsight, was the best thing you could do. I stuck to the couch, the corner near the fireplace, while my husband fed the fire.

Miles rolled in with Graham from Maryland, soon after my mother, Bob and my sister Caroline arrived. Miles and I would catch each other's eyes across the room like two people adrift on the sea. Then his friends came by and he was upstairs or gone.

Bob sat down on a table next to my corner and listened to me recount every detail of what I saw in the ER, everything, even the blood on my shoes, even the glow on my dead son's face. He sat still, watching my face, knowing he could say nothing to fix it, just like at Mount Sinai Hospital 25 years before. He sometimes reached for my hand, or gently shook his head, but he never looked away until I was done.

When the light turned to dark, they left to a nearby hotel and someone said I should sleep. I remembered that I had now not slept in about 30 hours. I lay back on the couch and closed my eyes.

There was a body, a young man's pale body pulled from a gurney to a stretcher, it jiggled and bounced the way a lifeless body moves, you know it after being a nurse for so many years, you say to yourself, *He's dead*, and you look up to see if anyone else knows this too, and if they've been around for a while, they show you with their eyes, *Yep, he's dead.*

Then there's a wallet, a card, a name, a cry. *That's my son!* And I am falling.

But now there is another voice that says, *No, no, no. That's not my son!*

My eyes snap open.

I can't. I can't. Someone help me.

My mother says, *Somebody do something!*

My husband drives to the ER and tells them I can't sleep.

He fills a prescription for Ambien and heads home. Around midnight I take one and fall asleep in the middle of a sentence. But at 4 a.m. my eyes open, my chest hurts, deep. I see the flash of a knife, a body on a stretcher. *No, no, no.*

I slow my breath. It was a dream, just a dream. My husband sleeps beside me as I sit up, the pain in the left side of my chest still radiating deep within me.

Oh God, this is not a dream. Spence...no, I can't, no, no, no. My eyes adjust to the dark, to my new life.

January 27th

Nothing in the House

Thy servant Lord, hath nothing in the house, Not even one small pot of common oil;
For he who never cometh but to spoil
Hath raided my poor house again, again,
That ruthless strong man armed, whom men call Pain.

– AMY CARMICHAEL

Mom came down the stairs as the sun was rising and saw me sitting on the couch.

"Let me make you some eggs, Bird," and she disappeared into the kitchen. There was food everywhere. Food and flowers – but it was disgusting to me. I hadn't eaten in two days and the nurse in me knew why I was starting to pass out every time I stood. I moved into the kitchen and watched my mother cook.

When I was little, when I would get really hurt, like when I broke my leg skiing, mom would draw me a hot bath, pour a little bourbon into a Dixie cup and set it on the toilet seat next to the bath.

"You can sip on that while you soak," she would instruct me, and the bitter fire from the paper cup would bring comfort to me as I lay naked and alone in the hot water.

Her scrambled eggs were the sober substitute I guess. They went down easy and I returned to the couch. The phone rang constantly and I gave my mother the job of screening calls, forgetting her hearing was bad.

"Who is it? Anthony? Danny?" She was getting agitated, and acting more like a Rottweiler at the door than a grandmother. She was mad at everyone, especially my husband. I had been married three times and it didn't matter who my husband was, she disliked them all. Then once they were gone she would speak fondly of them, like dear departed friends.

She glared at C.B. as he came in the door, after reading the Sunday paper and leaving it in his truck. I had given him instructions to keep all news away from me. We had already dealt with TV crews parked outside and reporters pressing us for a story. Tell them we want our privacy, I said.

C.B. also told them we had forgiven the killers. This simple statement put the brakes on all conversation that leaned towards revenge, or tearing at the character of the defendants and their families, at least around us. They had arrested five the day before, just as the cop promised and had a warrant out for one more who had run to Rhode Island.

The eggs were churning in my stomach. Jake and Miles were sleeping in and the day was moving forward. My husband came into the living room and smiled at me.

"You are a little too happy for me," I said.

"I'm not happy, Robin. I just know God's involved. He's gonna bring something good out of this."

"Romans 8:28. Thanks for the scripture reference," I snapped, then got up and headed into the bedroom, shutting the door. I climbed back into bed, curling up into a ball, pulling the covers up over my head. Darkness settled in, bringing thoughts I dared not ever ask.

What if God is not real? I was spinning, weightless, like a speck of dust.

What if this is a fairy tale I've chased for the last 14 years? What if I was wrong to pull my sons along with me, like a pied piper heading towards a cliff?

What if Spencer would be alive, would be happy, if I did it all different?

The questions enclosed about me, the darkness reached deeper and I felt sick that I had said them, even to myself. They coursed through my blood, leeching into my soul, leading me to a place that was black like velvet and still, where there were no more questions, no light and time stopped its awful march forward.

I'm done.

It's okay. Who can blame you? It's enough. You've had enough, the Darkness whispered.

Yes, enough, I agreed. *It's over.*

Then He came in. I felt Him at first, I felt the light before I saw anything, even though the darkness changed. He was bigger than the dark.

Robin. There was a pause.

Yes, I am here.

Robin, if you quit... He knows, of course He knows. I brace myself, curling up tighter.

I will still love you.

My breath catches. Exhale.

Then in the dark, I see a light, like the sun, coming up over a horizon. There's a road, silhouettes against the light, walking on the road. It looks hot and dry; dust explodes under their feet.

But if you leave your heart open, I can use it to bring people through.

Now I see faces, they are tired, thirsty, they look like pictures of refugees you see in the news, but it is not a huge crowd, just a steady stream, coming up over a hill and down this road. I watch for what seems a while, fascinated, not recognizing any face. Then I return to the question. Or was it a question?

Okay. I will. I lie still. Then He speaks again.

But if you open the door of your heart, you have to leave it open, all the way.

No opening and closing at my whim, and no half open door. Really, no door at all. I get it.

Okay, I will.

I threw the covers off, the fatigue washing over me, and sat on the edge of the bed. The sun was out. Still. I could hear my mother answering the phone.

"Who is this?" The anger framed each word. "I can't understand you!"

I stood, lightheaded at first, then took a few steps and opened the door.

C.B. went over to Spencer's car that morning, still parked outside the apartment complex and emptied it out, grabbing the small black Bible Spencer used that was tucked next the driver's seat. A plainclothes cop came over and asked him what he was doing. He introduced himself: Detective Chuck Peterson. He said he thought we had moved away because he hadn't heard Spencer or Miles' names come up in years.

Later on C.B. graciously took over the phone, and I sat next to him on the couch, watching the fire, receiving hugs from a steady stream of young men, most of them familiar, as they came through the house. But there was one call that made my husband sound different and I could see his face change, the brow furrow, the jaw tighten.

"Who is it?" I asked.

"It's Jermaine," and he was ready to hang up.

"I'll take that," I said, putting my hand out. C.B. sighed and handed the receiver to me.

"Hi Jermaine, it's Robin." I hadn't seen Jermaine in many years. Spence had dragged him to church on Easter a few years earlier. They sat behind me, and Spence was grinning like a kid at Christmas, but Jermaine was edgy, looking like he just got caught doing something bad, smiling at the girls, but not interested in much else. He never came back. Then Spence would run into him on the streets. The story was always the same; Jermaine was moving, or in trouble.

"Jermaine's gonna get killed some day," Spence had said just a few months earlier. He was standing in the kitchen, leaning against the counter with his arms folded, and it came out of the blue. I didn't know how to respond. I knew he still loved his old friend, the one who had given him the dumb tattoo using a needle and a Bic pen, the one he prayed for. Still I didn't like him being too close to him, or caring so much.

"Hi Jermaine," I said into the phone.

"I'm calling because you deserve to know the truth." His voice was low, a little hoarse, like he had just woken up. I said nothing, but held on to the phone.

"I take full responsibility for Spencer's death," he said next. "They were coming after me, they wanted me. It's my fault." Pause. My brain felt sluggish and muddled. It was difficult to understand people, like watching a movie with subtitles. Then he said,

"It's all over for me."

What – wait. I felt a nudge inside. *Pay attention here.* I sat up on the couch and tried to focus. I was losing him.

"Jermaine, I forgive you. But you need to know a greater forgiveness. You need to do what Spence wanted you to do all along." I was alert now, holding the phone tighter. "Don't let my son die in vain."

We talked for a while, Jermaine telling me about how he had been clean for six months once, how he and Spence had talked about church. I asked him to come to the funeral.

"I'll be there," he promised. I knew that his word was good, that it was a street thing, a matter of respect.

Later that week he stopped by to see Miles, and Miles handed him the only thing of Spencer's he had asked for when he came home from college – Spencer's Bible, the one C.B. had salvaged from his car.

Jermaine called twice more, assuring me he would be at the funeral and to introduce me to Arheesia, the girl who had been with Spence the night he died, who had held a towel to his chest waiting for rescue, as his breathing slowed then stopped. I could not understand her; she was sobbing softly, but with great heaving cries, unable to speak more than a word or two at once. And Jermaine, slipping in and out of street

slang, maybe high too, was indiscernible. I hung up and went
to lie down. My body felt like it was disappearing, my strength
fading to a desperate whisper. *I can't do this.*

> **Journal, 1/27/02**
> *Dear Lord,*
> *I have nothing. No strength, no courage, no understand-*
> *ing, not even assurance. Let not my faith falter too. I am*
> *afraid also of losing you. Forgive me Father, and help me.*

The next morning, C.B. came through the door with a
folded newspaper. He held it towards me, knowing he had to
explain fast.

"I think you should see this, Robin. I think God is in this
whole thing." He handed it to me and I unfolded it, doubtful.

Front page, Cape Cod Times:

"Killing may be case of wrong identity" A photo next to
this headline showed a family weeping, kids holding candles
next to an impromptu memorial that was made outside of the
apartment where the attack occurred.

The facts were sketchy. A party, a fight, another fight in
retaliation. Then a return retaliation, this time with blood in
mind, weapons in hand – a stick, a golf club, a crowbar and a
large kitchen knife. Two pit bulls even. Spence had not been
there, at the party, the fight. Where were you, Spencer? The
floor reeled beneath me, and then my eyes caught the subtitle
A Religious Respectful Person. I smiled, thinking how that
would make Spence chuckle. *Religious* was a term my church

mocked. *It's not about Religion,* we would hear over the pulpit, *it's about a Relationship with Jesus.*

But I knew the paper was giving a nod to Jesus, and to who Spence was. They had interviewed some of the people at the memorial, a large rock covered with pictures, Bibles, a basketball even, and in the neighboring apartments. They remembered him sharing the gospel, inviting them to church. He was known as a "youthful evangelist who would wander door to door, sharing his convictions but never pushing his beliefs on others."

Three days before he died he told his friend Jay, "Jesus was the best thing that ever happened to me."

"That conversation changed me," Jay admitted later.

Further down the article, these words:

"Despite his religious convictions, the South Yarmouth man remained close to former high school classmates who preferred the lure of late night parties to Sunday morning church pews."

"He didn't try to push religion on anyone, but he lived his life in a way that made you respect his beliefs," friend Jeff Mendoza said. "You couldn't ask for a more loving friend."

Jeff with the bloody towel to his head, in the ER that night. He must've been at the party and the first fight with Fat Joe. Sweet Jeff. Spence always had a soft place in his heart for the big shy boy that was now a man. He told me he was spending New Year's Eve with Jeff, and when I asked him why, he simply said, "Because I told him I would."

I gave the paper back, indifferent. What does it all matter anyway?

"I called the funeral home," C.B. said next. "We have an appointment at 11."

Spencer's body...where was it anyway? I had lost track. Just from working in the ER, I knew that homicides belonged to the state; they were literally evidence and we were taught to be careful with them. *Don't take out an ET tube or IV lines, and document, document, document!* And I had, I remembered now, carefully filling out the trauma sheet, and neatly drawing in the stab wounds. Then checking the box next to "Deceased," making sure the time was precise, my handwriting neat in the space provided.

But his body, where is it? Where are you, Spencer?

> *I thought that I had courage in the house,*
> *And patience to be quiet and endure,*
>   *And sometimes happy songs; now I am sure*
> *Thy servant truly hath not anything,*
> *And see my songbird hath a broken wing.*

– AMY CARMICHAEL, "NOTHING IN THE HOUSE"

We had an appointment at the funeral home, and we had to go, my husband said. I was angry because he had told the people Spence lived with to pack up his stuff, and I didn't want anyone to touch anything. Why did they have to do that, so fast, just pack him up like a show that's over? Boxes. Your life goes into boxes. My anger poured into a wider river of hysteria so that by the time we reached the funeral home I couldn't walk, I just leaned on the truck, sobbing.

"I didn't want them to touch anything! Why did they do that? I didn't want anyone to touch anything!" I couldn't stop.

C.B. was lost, unable to fathom an answer to my distress which was now uncontrolled, like a volcanic geyser surging into the air, so he closed his door and walked away.

"We're late. I'll be inside."

Several minutes later I entered the side door into a carpeted office with a large desk and several captains chairs around it. An older man in a dark suit pulled one out for me with a brief smile.

"We were not sure who you would choose. When we hadn't heard anything…"

His voice trailed off, implying we had taken a long time to choose a funeral home. I suppose they read the news, I thought. C.B. fielded the business end of things, which is considerable. Price, options. Chauffeur? No. Obituary? Yes.

He got out a pen and started to write, politely waiting for my answers.

Well, let's see. He was a carpenter and… Africa, Christian rap. Yes, he loved Jesus.

I'm writing my child's obituary.

The body, the stretcher, the tattoo.

No, no, that's not my son!

We were led down some stairs into a casket showroom. There were ornate ones, mahogany, maple, walnut. Spence would like the wood ones, but he wouldn't like the price, I mused. He had my practical, frugal side. *Scottish,* we would say. Why pay a lot for something you bury in the ground?

"I'll take this one," I said, touching the side of a plain metal casket. I could sense his disappointment as we headed back up the stairs.

"I just want you to know that we don't make any judgments here," he said as we shook hands by the door. *Judgments.*

I walked out to the truck, my mind gridlocked and exhausted. *Judgments?*

Somehow in the chaos of that first week, my mother got left with me. My brothers and sister returned to New York, all coming back up to the Cape for the memorial service and burial. They may have asked her if she wanted to be with me, or assumed that a mother would want to stay but they forgot who our mother was. Her instability was unraveling faster than mine. As calls came in and visitors trudged through the door, she regarded each intrusion with distrust. If I left the house, she stood staring at me, like my skirt was too short and I was headed to the wrong side of town. And typically my poor husband received the brunt of her rage.

In the meantime, I struggled to keep track of Jake. At one point, I found him lying on the couch, staring at the ceiling, his eyes tired and his jaw set to fight back tears.

"So we're not going skiing?" His nine-year-old mind was trying to grab onto something that could be added or subtracted, that could provide meaning to the mess around him.

"No, honey. We won't go skiing." *That was before, that was a whole different life ago.* I tried to hold him but he was limp and detached.

I thought back to 1964, when Timmy died, my eight-year-old view of the strange new world around me, of watching the steady stream of grownups through my home. I was invisible, except for an occasional pat on the head as I roamed past the crumpled tissues clutched in the hands that swung close to my face. I wanted the old world back, the simple one of play and all my family where they should be. Then, in time, I forgot what normal was.

In my mind, I was determined to make it different for Jake, to let him know I was there but I had almost forgot to send Jake to school two days in a row. I offered to let him stay home, but Jake wanted to go, to be around the dependable rhythm of a fourth grade classroom, somewhere he could breathe and play again.

C.B. had gone up to the courthouse, summoned by the DA's office. They had wanted me, but I had no interest in talking, so he went, returning with an armful of books and pamphlets.

"These are for you," he said. He laid them in front of me on the kitchen table, like travel brochures. I glanced at the booklet on top.

Homicide Survivors. I picked it up, the words slamming me in the head. That's you, Homicide Survivor. That doesn't even make sense – I did not survive a homicide, I thought. *Stupid idiots!* I could feel the anger shoot upward from somewhere deep. It was quick. The book flew through the air, smashing into the kitchen wall, landing in a disheveled heap on the floor. *Stupid book.* My husband picked it up and took it away.

I had to shop for clothes, for funeral clothes. It's a bad time of year to shop, I said to myself. And the rain wouldn't stop. My mother offered to help but historically we could never shop together. Memories of her collapsing into a chair at Bloomingdale's, depressed and weary while I spun in circles of indecision between the racks of new dresses, made the choice easy. I had to be alone.

At Macy's I found nothing, then looked up to see the face of a nurse I had worked with at the hospital for years, before I went to the ER. Turns out she was also shopping for an outfit to wear to my son's funeral.

"Oh!" She let out a little scream when she saw me, almost falling backwards into a clothes rack. "I didn't expect to see you here!"

I tried to smile, apologetically, seeing I had scared her. Then she was gone and I stared after her, remembering stories my mother had told me of women turning their shopping carts around in the market or crossing to the other side of the street. Now I could see them clear as day, how they might've let out a little scream too, leaving my mom feeling ashamed. I left the mall and went home.

That night the doorbell rang, the front door, which hardly ever gets used on Cape Cod. I opened it to find Thomas, poor Thomas from the ER, standing on the porch, in the rain. He had on a big coat, too big, and it was soaked through, the fake fur on the hood wet like an old dog. He said nothing, just stood there, his face twisted and tears mixed with rain.

"Thomas, oh Thomas!" I opened the door, but he stepped back. His shoulders were shaking, but he made no noise.

"Thomas, it's going to be okay, honey. Come in and get dry." I didn't care that I was getting wet too, as I pushed the storm door all the way open.

He stepped back off the porch, and turned into the rain, the night, looking back only once, the door still open as I watched him till he was gone.

One thing I can't describe: reading your child's obituary. At first I thought, *There's Spence!* And my heart did a little flip, like when you see your kid in a school play, or winning an award. The picture was nice. It was taken off a photo I took of him in South Africa. He has just a plain white shirt on, his face is tan from the African sun, and his look is sweet. Just a little embarrassed because mom is taking my picture, but also, *Hey I'm happy mom, right here, at this moment.* Content. In the full picture, a young African boy looks up at him with a wide grin on his face, but they cropped that out for the paper.

Spencer T. MacLeod, 21

I read on: a carpenter, a Christian, loved to rap, trip to South Africa, his family. My eyes stumble on "survived by" and I slowly lay the paper down on the bench next to me in the kitchen. I scan the page. **Obituary.** Then his picture. His name, then age: 21. That's all, 21 years. The stretcher, the tattoo, the wallet. *No, that's not my son.*

But the paper – **Obituary.**

I get up. There's a few things you can't describe.

Like getting dressed for your child's funeral. I didn't want to do the black thing. I found a pretty pale blue sweater and wore the necklace Spence gave me for Mother's Day, from him and Miles, who stood behind him as he handed me the dainty little bag with his carpenter's hands, smiling as I opened it, both of them knowing they had nailed it when they saw my delight at the pretty silk thread necklace strung with beads of wood and glass and pearl. Forget makeup.

Like watching a video about your son at his funeral, his life in photos, short clips of him playing basketball, rapping in

Africa, playing with lion cubs, skiing, holding his newest little sister from Cambodia, just last week, she had just arrived at his dad's house and he held her and brushed her fine hair with a little baby brush. He looked tired, but so tender towards her. I leaned back in my seat, in the front row of the church, next to Miles. I thought, *What a beautiful young man!* And my heart spread open, like any mother who was so proud of her boy, ready to soar.

To my left was the metal casket, the one I picked out, in the front of the church. It didn't look so bad with flowers all over it. A young man with dreadlocks stood close to it, weeping, his shoulders heaving. I wanted to comfort him, to tell him it's all right, but I never saw him before or since. People filled every seat, then stood in the back and along the walls. And I've never seen so many people, or so much food. I thought, *Spence would really love this, especially the food.*

You get hugged a lot. One guy hugged me so hard I heard my hair clip snap. I was there, but just barely. I knew how to breathe and smile and lift my hand to God. At the end, Pastor Campo asked if anyone wanted to make Jesus their Savior and I saw all kinds of people come down to the altar. Lots of people prayed and lots of people cried too. I didn't know most of the young people, but I saw Jermaine. He was kneeling on the floor with Sandy, Spencer's best friend from church, and Sandy had his arm around him. *Spence would really love this,* I thought.

Leaning up against the casket was a huge poster size picture, the same picture of him in Africa, with the small boy in it, looking up at the beautiful young man, who smiled at his mom taking the picture. Content. *I'm happy now, mom.* That's the only way I can describe it.

Next morning. The burial. I knew I had to get dressed, and I had to go to the funeral home – that was all. When we walked in, Shawn Kimball was there alone in the room with the casket, with a state trooper standing close by.

I had visited Shawn while he was in the hospital. He was the second stabbing victim that came into the ER right after Spence. His wounds were serious, and he was whisked off to the OR shortly after arrival. It was later that day, while he recovered in a hospital bed, that he found out Spence had died.

"He saved my life," he said. Then he wept. Shawn was the kind of kid that was always on the periphery of the in-crowd. He was smart but sensitive, and a little child-like, the kind of kid bullies were attracted to. He had done a brief stint in the military, and then came back to the instability of a home busted apart by drugs.

Shawn looked at me as I walked into the room. I could tell he had been crying.

"I just wanted to be here before everyone else," Shawn said. The trooper nodded at me with sad eyes, holding his hat in gloved hands, then looked at Shawn like it was time to go. We embraced, then I turned back to the room lined with chairs, the casket, having no idea that I would be standing there for the next three hours hugging 1200 people while they were ushered in one door and out another.

I was glad Miles stood next to me. C.B. and my mother were a little further down the line and I could sense my mother's edginess as the morning turned to afternoon and still people just kept coming. The funeral directors suggested we talk less and I guess that meant faster hugging. For years later, I assumed everybody wanted to hug me, so I would just open my arms when I ran into people, causing a few awkward moments when I assumed wrong.

It was cold, and the wind kicked up in great swirling gusts. A policeman saluted us as we made the turn at a sign that said Woodside Cemetery. Eight young men including Miles and Jermaine, pulled the coffin from the back of the hearse and carried it up a small hill, where a large green tent was set up. My legs felt funny, and I leaned into C.B. as we walked towards the tent. Then I saw it – the hole in the ground, a black rectangle cut into the bright green carpet covering the ground. The casket was placed right over it, a perfect fit.

No, I can't... I started towards the casket; to grab it before it went down into the hole, just tell them to stop all this, to go home, this is *not* my son, when Pastor Campo spoke.

"Spencer is not here." I stopped and looked at him. That's right. I looked up, like God would pull open the cloudless blue sky and say, "He's right here!" But the sky didn't change, not that I could tell.

After the reception where everyone stood around drinking soda and talking in low voices, I just wanted to go home. I was sick of people, all of them.

"Call me if you need anything!"

My son, I need my son.

The house was quiet and I noticed the drooping flowers in vases filled with murky water that smelled like decay. Food was scattered around the counter tops; casseroles, pies, unable to fit into the freezer. The house seemed to have stopped breathing, it was so quiet and suddenly I missed people, everyone.

It was late, when I remembered I had no more sleeping pills so I called my doctor who was of course not there. It was Saturday night. A covering doctor answered my call.

"Hello, I've run out of Ambien, I need more." Silence, which as a nurse I recognize as time for the doctor to gather ammunition.

"It will have to wait, I'm sorry," she stated firmly. "I don't know you, I can't just prescribe Ambien for anyone." I was incensed.

"My son died," I explained. "My son was murdered last week. The funeral was today…" I was grabbing at the air, and hearing how pathetic I sounded.

She interrupted. "I'm sorry. But I can't help you. You will have to go to the Emergency Room." The Emergency Room? My job? Where they brought my dead son's body?

"No thanks, no. Okay fine." I hung up. *Okay, I guess it's me and you, Jesus.*

I thought of a conversation I had had earlier in the day, at the reception. Someone had insinuated that perhaps God was slacking when Spence died. Like He just folded His hands and shook His head.

Sorry. I wish I could do something! With a little lame shrug.

"Sometimes things just happen and even God's hands are tied," they said and I felt the same rage rise inside of me.

"Either God is everything He says He is, or He's nothing at all," I blurted out, surprising myself. Everything -- Redeemer, Defender, Deliverer, the One who holds the world in His hands, the one I trusted to hold my son. He is Love everlasting.

Here's another thing I can't describe: I knew I had a long journey ahead, I knew I was alone. And I also knew I was not alone, that Jesus said He would never leave me or forsake me. But I could not hear Him, see Him or feel Him.

The sound of pain is louder than a jet taking off inside your head but quieter than a casket showroom. The color of pain is darker than black; you can't tell if you are standing up or upside down. It is spinning and spinning past everything familiar, where you once found comfort, into a dimension separate from life, without gravity or even a wall to lean against. You are outside but inside looking out. It absorbs all your senses, so that even taste is dead. And there's no time to stop and fix it or just wait for the lights to come up because time won't stop, not at all. It pushes you forward like some cruel soldier taunting you with his bayonet. *Get moving! If you stop you are dead.*

I thought about being dead a lot. How cool the ground would feel around me, the peace in the dark soil, in the place of rest. I would close my eyes and pretend I was asleep, like when I was a child. I would lie perfectly still and watch as people passed by and said,

"I knew her once but now she is no more."

2.

REVIVAL

For I know that my Redeemer lives —

– JOB 19:25 NKJV

There was Jermaine, then Mike, his brother Jeff, their mom. Then other guys started showing up at church too, maybe out of curiosity, maybe it was something deeper. Stories in the paper continued, arrests were made and the word "forgive" had been spoken across church pews, TV stations, bars and the smoky dim pockets of poverty and violence.

They came in, sometimes filling up rows near the front, smelling of cigarettes, sometimes liquor, oversized winter coats stuffing the chairs, and God met them, face to face. They were mostly young men, many I recognized from Spencer's past, and later, I would find in his journals, on prayer lists. I loved to hug them and many nights cook for them, easing a bit of the emptiness; to make huge pots of chili and pans of gooey brownies and watch their eyes grow big like it was Christmas.

Many came just to see if it were true, that Jermaine was "for real," that he had really given his whole mess to Jesus; that he changed. Some, like Brandon, Mike and Murph stayed, and they changed too. Impromptu Bible studies sprang up in different homes, drawing many more out, some just wondering, some desperate -- and Jesus met them there, and they were never the same.

I liked to sit several rows behind them. It was like I could just see heaven leaning over the balcony, and saying, "Look!"

Some of Spencer's friends from church went out and found more. It was like fishing in a stocked pond. The memorial in Swan Pond Village was well attended every night; more Bibles, pictures, cards spread out around the large rock. Police tape waved in the breeze around the busted door and smashed window of the now-empty apartment. Kids milled around, singing, crying, looking for answers.

Spencer had become a street hero of sorts. A Boston Herald article described him as an "evangelist" who had "recently turned to Jesus and was preaching the gospel". C.B. and I had refused to be interviewed by the media and simply asked for our privacy. So they went elsewhere. The memorial was one of the first stops.

It was January, it was cold. Sometimes C.B. and I would drive through, waving at the kids, some adults. My part was to cook, to watch with a little bit of wonder at what God would do.

One night I invited Shawn Kimball and Jermaine over for lasagna and broccoli just because you have to have something green on the plate. Shawn was a no-show, which inflamed Jermaine, and after a few calls on his cell phone he said, "I'll be right back."

Twenty minutes later, he pushed Shawn through the door into the kitchen.

"Sit down and eat Spencer's mom's broccoli," Jermaine said, as he steered Shawn to the table with the sleeve of his coat. I felt bad for Shawn, for the broccoli I knew he would eat so I loaded his plate with lasagna and tried to smile but he looked down, sheepishly, and pulled in his chair.

Later, we would sit on my couch and I would listen to him tell me about his wounds, his arm, his back and abdomen, both of us pushing away the elephant in the room, Spencer bleeding to death on a dirty carpet, my son, his friend, right before his eyes.

3.

SPRING

Grief is not a disease. It is not an illness. It is not depression.
Grief is, in fact, an expression of love. Grief can only
be a disease if love is.

– DR. JOANNE CACCIATORE

There was something about the crocuses that took me down. It seemed so silly, even then, but you get used to the small things coming around like a left hook from nowhere, like seeing a favorite cereal or the car they used to drive. But the crocuses, they just looked so frail, about four of them leaning into the chimney right outside in the melting snow. I forgot that time would move on, that seasons pass, and I was not ready.

Miles had tried to help me sort through Spencer's stuff on his spring break. Socks and underwear were thrown out, although I put his good wool socks aside for C.B.. We culled our favorite t-shirts, sweaters, hats and what Miles did not want went into a blue plastic bin. Notebooks, sketchpads, journals, calendars marked up with Spencer's lists – these were all premium keepsakes. But most of his pens, markers, broken oil pastels were tossed. Ink bottles with calligraphy pens – find someone who wants them. Tools; keep. Worn out pillowcase – toss. Photographs, stacks of them – save. I could feel myself disconnecting but I tried to stay attentive as Miles went through box after box, because I knew he was trying hard to be efficient.

After he left I stuck my face into Spencer's clothes hanging in the closet and inhaled, still catching a scent; sweat mixed with salt air and wood, a young man's scent, earthy but sweet. Then I went into the garbage and pulled everything out.

The crocuses were purple with gold tongues, audacious in the gray landscape of a Cape Cod spring. I stared at them for a minute, then burst into tears, and stood crying on my little porch in the cold March air. I felt certain that God would take away this pain, that things should hurt less, not more, but this was a bad sign. A new season was turning, bearing down like a bully, and I could feel the push from behind as I dug in.

Every day I drove down to the cemetery, got out of the car and walked over to the small plaque, the rectangular scar healing slowly in the worn winter grass where a casket had been swallowed up just weeks before.

Spencer MacLeod
1980-2002

No, no that's not my son, I would say to the plaque, then I'd look up into the trees, the sky and wait for God to send me back home again.

Sometimes I'd walk to the library and sit in a corner with a magazine, turning the pages, the words foreign and stupid, bouncing off my eyes back to the page. Then I'd get up and pick out a book and repeat the same process. Every book, every paper, every conversation went the same way; a stretcher, a body, a tattoo. *That's not my son, no – it's not.*

I remember so clearly the first time I dug my face into his pillow that I kept upstairs in the closet – and he was gone. His scent had vanished. All I could smell was an old musty pillow stuffed with dead feathers. Then I grabbed his clothes, his sweater, his shirts, burrowing into them, inhaling, my breath deep and desperate. Vanished. The last wisp of his presence here on earth, gone. *No, no, please God.* I fell down into the closet, sobbing, pulling his shirts on top of me.

But he was gone.

4.

ROSIE THE RESCUE DOG

I got Rosie just about three weeks after Spence died. I admit I felt a little funny about it, like people might think I was trying to replace my son with a dog. But it was Jake's idea – he had announced that he wanted a guard dog. He was acting fearful, especially at night, asking my husband and me to lock all the windows, secure the house. I thought that he may have overheard some of the violent details of Spencer's death, how the door was broken down and it made me sad for him so I felt a guard dog was reasonable. Jake told me only recently that it wasn't the home invasion that spooked him. It was watching scary movies at a neighbor's house.

The paper was advertising lab-mix puppies and I found Rosie in a basement, one of four left in a large box. She was sleeping in the corner, oblivious to the puppy ruckus around her. I picked her up and held her to me and I swear this is true – she put her arms around my neck and hugged me.

I brought our new guard dog proudly into Jake's fourth grade classroom and he graciously allowed every child in the class to maul his new dog as Rosie tried her best to sleep through it all. I could tell even then he was a bit skeptical about her guarding skills but I assured him she would get real big.

In those early days when the pain was so heavy, waking up was the hardest part of the day. Sleep was dark and haunted then I would open my eyes to the worst nightmare ever. I could hear Rosie getting restless in her crate and I would dress quickly and run out of the house with her. I don't know why I had to run, but something propelled me forward, as if I was being chased.

We would walk and walk until we reached water and I would cry and talk to God or yell at God while Rosie splashed and chased frogs and cormorants. In blizzards, in soaking rain, in blasting heat we would not miss a morning together. I would often pass an older gentleman walking also and he nicknamed me "Miss Faithful" because we were out in every kind of weather. Now I wonder if he was walking off a loss too.

Rosie got big but she never became a guard dog. She was so good natured she looked like she was going to bust out laughing when she saw a stranger. Even the UPS man played with her. If another dog attacked her, she just laid down and looked at me like I was the guard dog.

Someone told me once that the name "Rose" means "divine love" and then it all made sense. Rosie was not a guard dog; she was a Rescue Dog, sent just for me, to rescue me from the dark terror I woke up to each day. She got me up; she got me out the door and to a place where I could meet up with God. She saved me. And she was Miss Faithful too.

5.

MEETINGS

Yarmouth Fire Department. It was addressed to Spencer Macleod, and inside was a bill for $900. I guess I laughed. He had gotten a bill from the ER also, and when I called and asked what I should do with it, the chief ER doc said, "Tear it up and throw it in the trash."

The Fire Department was right down the road so I took a walk. I thought it would be a good opportunity to talk to some of the medics who had been there that night, who had been with Spence.

I could hear the loose banter of the guys as I walked through the door, then as they saw me, a couple of them stopped and stood straight. One medic, the one I recognized from the trauma room with the papers in his hand, turned away.

"Hi, I'm Spencer Macleod's mother...the one who..."

"Yes ma'am, can we help you?" An older EMT stepped towards the counter as the room emptied out.

"I, I was just wondering if there was someone who was there that night, someone I could talk to..." He seemed to be holding his breath as he looked down at me. "And I have a

bill…" *Show him the bill; help him breathe for cryin' out loud.*
I handed it to him and he took another deep breath as he
scanned it.

"Let me see if the chief is in," he said, turning to the
phone. I could see faces in the next room, peaking around the
door, their voices clipped and low.

The EMT hung up and moved back to the counter, ges-
turing to the left.

"Just go up those stairs, ma'am. The chief will talk to you."

As I climbed the carpeted stairs I looked behind me, and
the man was gone.

At the top there was an open door, and as I quietly stuck
my head around the corner I heard a voice call, "Come in!"

I looked in the direction of the voice and still saw nothing,
so I walked a few steps in, cautiously looking side to side.

"Over here!"

It was then I caught the cap, a large captain's hat, a little
reminiscent of Captain Kangaroo, and the face of the fire chief
beneath it. His eyes were clear and seemed to be smiling even
though his mouth was not. He was leaning to the left, out
from behind a large computer monitor. The room was large,
surrounded by windows, and he was alone in the midst of
stacks of paper piled on various file cabinets and desks.

"Oh hi!" I was nervous. "I, uh, got this bill, and I was
wondering…" The bill looked pretty rough by now, from my
folding and unfolding it a dozen times.

"I'll take that," he said and I stepped forward to hand it
to him, then back again, waiting. It was quiet. His head had
disappeared again behind the monitor, although now I could
see the top of his hat, the white with the gold amulet out of
place in the messy office.

"So your son was a Christian?" Surprised by the question, I stared at the black monitor back, then answered to it.

"Yes, yes he was."

Now the face poked out again, the eyes locking onto mine, a hint of a smile.

"Then you'll see him again," he stated matter-of-factly, holding my eyes for a moment – then he was gone again. I stood there, in the light of the big room, letting the words take their place, knowing I had to stop and think about something; that truth and trust and faith have to be matter-of-fact.

"Yes, I will," I said. That seemed to be the end of things so I slowly turned to leave, then remembered why I was there.

"The bill, I can…"

"It's taken care of." One last time he peeked around the computer. "Have a good day." The smile widened just a bit under the tall hat. I was dismissed and turned to leave.

At the bottom of the stairs, Sue, a paramedic, was waiting for me.

"Hi Robin," she said, smiling at me. "I was there, I was with your son."

We walked out into the early spring air and found a step to sit on in the sun. I thanked her for being willing to talk. It hadn't occurred to me that this was hard for them, and I was getting it. Sue rode in the ambulance with Spencer that night.

"He was so pale," she began. "I knew by looking at him that there was no blood in him. I knew…" She trailed off, knowing that as a nurse I could catch a lot of what she was saying, how you hope sometimes but you just know.

"I couldn't stop looking at how beautiful he was," she continued, looking off into that night, the chaos of police and rescue and detectives and the blood, all the blood. "There was something so peaceful about his expression," she said, then turned slightly to me, to make sure I could hear, waiting for the right words.

"Angelic. He looked angelic."

We talked a little longer; I would not push her for more than she was willing to say.

"I have kids. Two. After something like this, I look at them different. A lot of things are different," she said.

She walked me to my car and hugged me. I would see her again at the murder trial over a year later, to testify. I told her I was sorry she had gotten pulled into court.

"No, it's something I want to do," she said grabbing my hand.

Later I heard she moved away, I heard she was doing something else.

In May I was summoned to the District Attorney's office, located in the Barnstable Superior Courthouse. I was familiar with the smaller and more modern courthouses behind it; the Circuit Courthouse held the Juvenile Court in the basement, and I had spent many hours there, slumped against a wall, waiting for either Spencer or Miles to be called in.

Across the parking lot was the Probate Court, and I had also done time on those benches while a divorce was mediated with Jake's dad. The lawns and steps were dotted with people, mostly smokers, some in heated discussion, waving arms. Others sat alone on benches, exhaling smoke and staring at the patchy grass.

Susan, the Victim Witness Advocate, greeted me as I stepped off an ancient elevator, and guided me to her office. Multiple chairs and couches lining the walls obscured her desk, even though it sat almost in the middle of the room, piled high with folders. A tall window looked out onto the yard. The leaves on the oaks were just beginning to uncurl, fragile and pale.

Susan looked a little older than me, had the well-hewn look of a professional, but with eyes that were warm and searching. She kept the conversation going, listing the Assistant District Attorney's many accomplishments as she pulled chairs around and shuffled some folders.

"He'll be right in," she said, glancing again at the chairs, then the clock on her wall.

Rob Welsh was a stocky man of average height, mid-thirties I guessed. He had close-cropped hair and sensitive blue eyes. Susan told me he had been in the Army, piloting helicopters, and came from a long line of judges. Mentally I ran through the several I had stood in front of and wondered if any were related. When he walked in and shook my hand, he pulled a straight back chair into the middle of the room so that he could be closer to me, but still at a distance. Under his arm was a large file.

He had details, all the details of Spencer's murder. As he sat there and spoke in a soft voice, occasionally looking up at me, then looking at his papers, I wondered how he would look in a crowded courtroom trying to prosecute a homicide. Lawyers always seemed like a fraternity to me; loud and entitled, clicking wine glasses after a case and slapping each other on the back, like a courthouse form of jocks in a locker room. My mind wandered to the windows. It was raining.

"So the reason I am pursuing a first-degree murder charge…"

Susan walked in and out of the office like a nervous mother.

"They continued to beat Spencer, even after he was stabbed…"

I could feel my breathing speed up, and I needed to walk, maybe run. I shifted in the large upholstered chair.

"The trial may not take place for at least six months."

No, I can't do this. I sat forward in the chair, signaling my time was up. Rob stopped talking and shuffled the papers around in his lap, then looked briefly at me. *He cares,* I thought. That's why it's hard for him to look at me.

Any questions?

I asked for a copy of the file and he and Susan exchanged looks.

"I can't do that. It's not allowed." He said it gently but I felt embarrassed suddenly. Why would I even want that? Susan gave me some more pamphlets about homicides and what to expect and led me back to the elevator, assuring me they were there for me if I needed anything.

I need my son.

I threw the pamphlets into the car and drove home, past the lovely homes of Cape Cod, forsythia and daffodils splashing yellow into the gray. It didn't matter, it all looked ridiculous. God, I'm tired.

They stopped and picked up a crowbar, a golf club and a large stick.

Jake had a Little League game. I knew C.B. was there watching.

Then they drove to a house to pick up two pit bulls.

I pulled into the field. The concession stand was busy; parents stood in line, laughing, sharing stories, normal stories, not like my stories.

They saw Shawn through the window and parked outside.

I could see C.B. in the stands, cheering the team, excited, clapping and yelling. I had to tell him, I had to tell someone.

They broke the door down; it came off the hinges. Then they went in…

I was almost running when I got to the bleachers.

"Hi honey!" C.B. flashed a smile.

"I just came back from meeting with the Assistant DA. He told me everything, he…"

The sound of a bat cracking hit the air, and C.B. turned to the field. "Whoa! Look at that! A home run!" He jumped to his feet and pumped his fist in the air. I started to back away.

He looked at me and saw. "Oh honey, I'm sorry. What were you saying?"

I was running, I could hear him calling, but I was gone. I was running. Where do you run? Where can I go, God? There is no place I can escape to.

Spencer came down the stairs and tried to stop the attack.

My baby, my baby. I jumped in the car and sped off, the pamphlets Susan gave me sliding to the floor. There is nowhere to run.

Journal: May 17th, 2002

Met the prosecuting attorney yesterday and it all threw me back into the same darkness, the horror and evil of it. Oh Lord deliver me out of that furnace of pain, I can't bear it anymore.

Spencer, is it unbelievably lovely where you are? I wish you could just wave to me. No more pain for you. I wish for me. I love you and miss you always.

6.

THE BAPTISM

And now why are you waiting? Arise and be baptized, and wash away your sins, calling on the name of the Lord.'

– ACTS 22:16 NKJV

I could hear the singing through the woods, so I started to run across the parking lot, the Flax Pond picnic area, carpeted with a spongy layer of pine needles, then down the trail towards the pond. Once I saw the crowd, I slowed down, feeling foolish for running and being out of breath.

Those that were being baptized stood in a loose line that went from the water all the way up the sandy beach to the benches. Young guys and girls wore t-shirts and shorts and a towel mostly over their shoulders, nervously joking, their voices loud, blending with the banter of the church people lining the benches, who had turned their attention to the two men out in the water up to their waists, waiting.

I searched the crowd. Miles said he would come. I knew it was hard for him.

"I feel like it's Spencer's church, not mine," he had said, searching for an honest explanation as to why he skipped church when he could.

C.B. and Jake sat down near the beach. Jermaine and a few of the other guys saw me and waved. It was a perfect Memorial Day, extraordinary for Cape Cod, which usually threw cold rain down upon the hoards of tourists that had envisioned a picnic on the beach.

Then I saw Miles, up in the woods, actually right where I was but directly across the beach. We caught each other, our eyes holding a look that can only convey joy and sorrow at once, with a little nervousness too. I smiled. It really was funny we had both picked a place hidden but with the best view.

Then they were called forward into the water one by one, giving their name, their story, before the two men gripped them by the shoulders and pulled them backwards, down under the water in the name of the Father, the Son and the Holy Spirit. When they came up, cheers exploded from the crowd as the new believers, drenched, dripping and full of joy, made their way back to the beach and their waiting towel.

I wondered if Spence could at least get a list, like roll call, if he was leaning over the Book of Life, maybe looking over an angel's big shoulder.

"Hey," he'd say, "there's Jermaine and Murph! I prayed for those guys! Look at Jay! And his brother Larry! And there's Mike too! Wow, this is amazing!" And the angel would just look back at him with great patience and a little humor too.

I thought of Spencer's baptism with Miles in a pond when they were around 9 and 11. Old enough to know they needed to be forgiven, that they wanted what only Jesus could give them. Then Spence was baptized again at a teen boot camp after he came back to Jesus.

I'm serving the devil notice, he had said. And the devil heard it too. But he doesn't win, I thought, watching 27 people go down in the water that day. It doesn't cancel the pain or even answer why, I thought looking at Miles across in the woods, his expression so vulnerable and raw. But it serves the devil notice, yes it does.

The crowd cheered with each baptism and testimony, but I knew the noise was nothing compared to the shouts of praise in heaven that day.

Spencer is complete now, Pastor Campo had said, and somehow I knew that was true.

'The conqueror shall be clad in white raiment; I will never erase his name from the book of Life, but will own him openly before my Father and before his angels.'

– REVELATION 3:5 MOFFAT NT

7.

VALLEY OF BACA
(WEEPING)

Give sorrow words; the grief that does not speak whispers
the o'er-fraught heart and bids it break.

– WILLIAM SHAKESPEARE

I never did get Miss Eagan, the nice teacher Timmy had hoped for us in fourth grade. Back in the 60's, a parent never would've asked for a certain teacher for a child. You just got what you got, and you were expected to deal with it. I got Miss Cardosa.

"Cardosa is Portuguese," she announced to us the first day of school, and I had never heard of such a thing. I knew the I-talians lived on the other side of the Post Road, that they were loud and gregarious, crammed into small houses that were built for the WWII soldiers when they came back and were newly married - a starter home. But the Italians stuffed 13 kids in those at a time. They had built the railroad, my dad said, and just stayed around, apparently growing kids.

Anyway, we all just stared at Miss Cardosa, blinking. No one said a word about Portuguese, so I didn't feel so dumb. Then she asked us all what we did for the summer. A boy in the back that I had never seen raised his hand.

"Yes?" Miss Cardosa nodded to the boy.

"Timmy Gulian died," he blurted out. "And that's his sister!" He half stood in his seat so he could point at me, a few rows ahead. The room bristled with uneasy laughter and chairs scraping on the floor as the kids turned to see who he was pointing at. I smiled at the boy, then turned to Miss Cardosa, because I wanted to talk about it too. I had a lot to share.

"Quiet!" she thundered over our heads. The room stiffened.

"I know," she said. Then she scanned the room, taking in every scared look with a half smile. "And we will *never* talk about that again!" She avoided me and I could feel my face burn. I slumped down in my seat, hoping the kids weren't still looking at me.

I wanted to say *It's okay*, I wanted to say, *Please let me speak, let me say, I miss my brother and this is all a mistake because we were supposed to be in Miss Eagan's room, like twins. We were supposed to be together.*

But the words were gone now, falling to the ground, the words had to be buried and forgotten. It was the first day of fourth grade, and I already knew I didn't like anything about it.

Outside, the leaves turned their bellies to the sun, tired of summer, of holding on. I knew my brother was dead, but now I knew he was gone.

> *"An odd by-product of my loss is that I'm aware of being an embarrassment to everyone I meet. At work, at the club, in the street, I see people, as they approach me, trying to make up their minds whether they'll 'say something about it' or not. I hate it if they do, and if they don't. ...Perhaps the bereaved ought to be isolated in special settlements like lepers."*

> – C.S. LEWIS, *A GRIEF OBSERVED*

At first, I thought God would take the pain away. After all, he took my son away, and seated at the large cosmic bargaining table, I was trying to make a deal. It was pathetic.

People say a lot of dumb things but the one that topped them all was, "I don't know how you do it! I could never go through what you're going through!"

What are the options, I sometimes asked, when etiquette was swept aside. Suicide? Considered it. Drugs? Alcohol? Thought of that too. I admit, I recalled with fondness the warm burn of bourbon sliding down my throat, or maybe the dull softness of a sedative, like Ativan or Valium tamping down the sharp edge of pain; it all felt reasonable to consider, but again, I could not begin to fool myself. I would want more, and once the door opened just a crack, I would not be able to close it any more than you could stop a tsunami. I knew better.

In the morning I would run down to Bass River, Rosie leading the way, until I stopped at the river's edge and I would shout at the sky.

"This makes no sense! Why am I here?" The clouds edged across the sky, ignited by the rising sun as Rosie chased minnows.

"I don't want to be here," I would yell into the air. The sun would lift up over the opposite shore, the large modern homes framed into the pale blue curtain of the new day. I hated the new day, the sound of people waking, cars whooshing over the bridge that spanned the river. But I hated the night too, the images jolting me awake, more tears, my heart crumpled in agony.

God would not cut a deal. God did not even show up. There was no way out of this. I would turn from the sky, and with Rosie running ahead, run home again.

6/23/02 JOURNAL

Waves of sickening depression, felt melancholy at church, like everyone else is getting on with the business of life. And I am stuck on this wheel that just seems to go round and round. I am up then going down, getting ready to submerge I hold my breath until I come up. I hate it. I hate this existence and I can't pretend that I'm not just a little mad about this "cross to bear." I am sick of myself so I'm sure everyone else must be. Should I just learn to pretend?

Spencer's headstone finally arrived in August, and my mother drove up from New York to see it. A pickup truck pulled into the cemetery with it roped into the back. The stone guy looked disappointed that we were there waiting.

"I have to pour the slab," he said, as if we would understand how gravestones are commonly placed. We nodded dumbly, then moved to the bed of the truck where we could see the stone.

It was a unique color – so different, this guy almost had me believing that he drove to Vermont himself and cut it out of a mountain using chisels. Months had passed, the poor little grave was marked by a small plate from the funeral home that was blistering in the sun, and some potted plants. Somebody was walking off with the potted plants until I left a note that said,

Please stop stealing plants off my son's grave. God is watching you.

Then it stopped.

Mom sighed and touched the letters. "It's just beautiful, Bird," she said softly.

> *Spencer Timothy MacLeod*
> *Feb. 19, 1980 – Jan. 26, 2002*
> *Well done good and faithful servant*
> *Enter into the joy of the Lord*

The stone was left rough on the top and sides. I remembered that my mom had intentionally done that with Timmy's grave, "because he was a rough little boy," she had said. Spencer was just short of 22, a young man's prime, a carpenter, strong with rough hands.

Enter into the joy…

I was envious, and at times a little mad at him for going before me.

I could see him, before the throne, arms wide in worship, face turned upward in wonder and awe. He never understood how God could love him. Now he does.

Well done...

We oohed and aahed a few minutes more, then left the tired stone man to finish his work. Mother and daughter, taking one last look at the name, the stone and the grave, got into the car and drove through the field of stones and bones. We both knew there was nothing to say, and for a change, it was just fine. Deep calls to deep – the language of loss can't be heard.

As summer ebbed, Miles returned to college, and I was relieved to send him away from the Cape. His friends, the tight-knit circle of kids who grew up with some of the guys arrested for Spencer's murder, were good kids who cared about Miles, but the machismo allegiance was like a tinder box waiting for a spark.

C.B., Jake and I took off for the Adirondacks with my brother Graham and his family, to the mountains. We had never been there before and it was good to be with people that I didn't feel I had to perform for, in a place unfamiliar. Everyone in my family laughs loud, and a lot, and I liked being near it. I just couldn't join in.

A dense bubble of pain carried me through each day, filtering people, conversation and the landscape around me. I looked up to the magnificent sky at night, stars bursting through the black canopy and felt only sorrow. It was as if I was under the influence of a drug that would not allow me to see, hear, or feel anything other than pain, deep and haunting. I felt restless like an animal trapped in a cage, closer to death than life and tired of attempting escape.

There were times when Jake would be talking to me and I would hear his voice coming through the filter, "Mom, hello? Are you there?" and I would focus on the little face looking up into mine.

"Why do you keep shaking your head?" he asked me once, and I realized the other voice had become so much a part of me, I didn't even notice it any more, like the sound of breaking waves. *No, no, no...that's not my son.*

I drifted through the days, tethered to C.B. or my brother like a child prone to wander. We hiked, we swam, we laughed and Jake loved being with his cousins.

"You're having a hard time, aren't you sis," Graham asked, catching me outside looking at the sky.

"Yeah." I smiled. It felt good just saying it, like telling a secret we both knew. I breathed in the cool air and looked up again, past the dark mountains, the trees reaching into the night.

"The stars are amazing," Graham said softly, his face turned up with mine, just like the night our big brother died and we sat huddled close on our front porch, looking up. We seemed no bigger now under the immense northern sky, but we both knew for sure He was there; the One who strings the stars across the heavens, and the One who was with me, not just close but there, within the pain.

God can thunder in the whirlwind or call your name through the fire, but sometimes you can hear Him best when He says nothing at all.

8.

GOOD COURAGE

*And thine ears shall hear a word behind thee, saying,
This is the way, walk ye in it, when ye turn to the
right hand, and when ye turn to the left.*

– ISAIAH 30:21 KJV

I don't remember when I started the Board of Hope. It was a plain corkboard, and one day under sudden inspiration, or maybe desperation, I stuck a few things to it; notes, cards, a song and some scripture. I stood it up on my dresser so that when I walked by it, I would remember I was connected to the world – through friends, family, preachers and poets.

Courage. It was clipped to a piece of stationary with a little birdhouse on it and "A note from Marian Murray" printed across the top, then the familiar scrawl; hands that must've been 80 and arthritic, hands that worked and knew the currency of life – cleaning fish, culling through the black Edisto soil for potatoes and covered with chalk in a one room schoolhouse. She loved anything that could grow. She had loved Spencer too.

Courage is the basic virtue on which all others depend for vitality and life.

As I read the words, I retraced the surprise I felt when I opened her letter. Amid a flood of flowery Hallmark sympathy notes, the word *Courage* had leapt out at me, and I wasn't sure I liked it. Courage? But it was Marian so I had held the message tighter.

Of what use is wisdom if one hasn't the courage to act wisely?

Of what value is love if one hasn't the courage to love?

Of what value is truth if one hasn't the courage to speak it?

Of what consequence is faith if one hasn't the courage to embrace it?

There was no signature, no wrap up, no "praying for you" or "May the Lord etc. etc." Then on a page stapled to this were three scriptures.

We are pressed on every side by troubles, but we are not crushed or broken. We are perplexed, but we do not give up and quit. 2 Corinthians 4:8

Be strong and courageous. Do not be terrified; do not be discouraged, for the Lord your God will be with you wherever you go. Joshua 1:9

There was that word again – be *courageous.* I was intrigued. Then lastly,

I waited patiently for God to help me; and He listened and heard my cry, He lifted me out of the pit of despair. Psalm 40:1-2

Reading again this unusual sympathy note, I realized how much I needed these words. She was taking me by the shoulders, and in an amazing act of love and rescue, shaking me and pointing upward. She was correcting my posture.

Marian came to visit me in June 2002, five months after Spence died. Her knees were bad but she would only let me help her down the stairs. She had never been to Cape Cod; maybe even Massachusetts. We drove along the Old Kings Highway, comfortable with silence, distracted by the rambling roses and lilacs. I was still stunned and exhausted with the daily work of grief. She was in her eighties, her presence there was all that had to be said.

I drove her to Logan airport at sunrise. I don't remember if we ever said "I love you" but watching her disappear into the airport, small and frail, I knew she had to love me a lot. Less than a year later she died peacefully, pneumonia finally overtaking the "lousy lungs" she endured since childhood.

"I don't know if I'm more of a grandmother, or mother or just friend to you," she remarked once while we picked tomatoes in the full Carolina sun, sweat dripping off my face onto my dusty hands.

"Maybe all of them," I suggested, and we laughed, an easy laugh that Marian taught me. A laugh that is not afraid.

Thumbtacked nearby was a card from my brother, Graham with a little girl sitting on a couch, the words "Two ears, no waiting" across the top. He called every week, and when he asked, "How are you doing?" I knew he really wanted to know.

I think there is a passage in the Bible where Jesus says God puts us through the fire to be pure gold. I see you coming out of the fire as a pure, burning example of God's word in the world.

I did not feel like I was an example of anything other than some morose figurehead of tragedy. I could sense a roomful of people seize up when I entered.

"How *are* you?" I was asked, the smile fixed and wide as if they were coaching me through a script I hadn't fully memorized. Then I would get it.

"*Fine!*" My smile would match theirs, indicating we were through, and the topic would change. It wore me out.

The only company I could stand was my dog, my cat and a handful of close family and friends. And they were, not coincidently, the only ones who could stand me. Yet as time moved forward, even the best people fell away. They get tired, I reasoned. Who would stay in this parched and desolate land if they didn't have to? Still, as the year pushed forward, the pain did not get better, it only gained new dimension, and loneliness magnified the futility of waking up each day.

Also tacked to the Board of Hope was a square scrap of paper I copied from a book, a portion of a letter written by Samuel Rutherford to a young mother who had lost a daughter, circa 1700's. Rutherford was a fiery Scottish preacher who had buried two children.

Grace rooteth not out the affections of a mother, but putteth them on His wheel who maketh all things new, that they may be refined; therefore sorrow for a dead child is allowed to you, though by measure and ounceweights; the redeemed of the Lord have not a dominion or lordship over their sorrow and other affections, to lavish out Christ's goods at their pleasure.... The cup ye drink was at the lip of sweet Jesus, and He drank of it... Ye are not to think of it a bad bargain for your beloved daughter that she died – she hath gold for copper and brass, eternity for time. All the knot must be that she died too soon, too young, in the morning of her life; but sovereignty must silence your thoughts.

It seemed a bit harsh to me at first; "sorrow for a dead child is allowed to you, but by measure and ounceweights." Yet I knew I needed this truth, that my view had to be high, eternal, up over cemeteries and boxes of clothes that would never be worn again; that there was a scale outside of my vision and understanding that the Creator of time used, weighing each prayer, each cry from the hidden darkness of every soul, each life pronounced "worthless." He held it up to the light, and would marvel at its beauty, every tear he would count and bottle, and at night He would sing over the still darkness down below, sometimes songs of sorrow and grief, sometimes he would burst forth in joy with the birds and trees and wind singing along.

And then other times He calls His children home, knowing the violent tearing, the *Why* He cannot tell, is splitting your heart wide open.

"And a sword will pierce through your own soul too," Mary was told, when Jesus was just a fat little baby, eyes ablaze with joy at the sight of his mama. I looked it up. *Sword* meant a sword, as in a spear.

In time, in His time, the scale tips, and He pours His glory forth; a trickle at first, then a steady stream that eddies into a mighty river. A little weighs a lot. The black despair that extends beyond sight or reach, the coffin, the stone, the tears that pour forth without reason, begin to lift – up, up, up. Look up! His portion was becoming mine.

Rutherford continued: *The goods are His own. The Creator of time and winds did a merciful injury (if I may borrow the word) to nature in landing the passenger so early.*

Over time, the Board acquired more cards, a song, poems, including one Spence wrote called "Our Hope." As I passed it every day, I could feel something inside settle. It was the right way, the path upward. Hope. Simple, not easy, but simple.

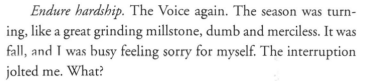

Endure hardship. The Voice again. The season was turning, like a great grinding millstone, dumb and merciless. It was fall, and I was busy feeling sorry for myself. The interruption jolted me. What?

I knew the scripture, somewhere in 2nd Timothy. The young preacher is getting ready to run for his life with the rest of the flock as Nero's torches were licking at his neck.

Endure hardship like a good soldier was the Apostle Paul's counsel. Timothy must've felt like I did. What's the use?

But I knew it was God trying to point me to something. It was hard, and He knew it would be. *Endure hardship.*

Autumn brought a cool breeze as the marsh grass faded to straw and the leaves scraped across the street in a gust of wind.

I can't share a hot apple cider with my son anymore.

I can't cook a Thanksgiving feast for him and watch his eyes light up at a pumpkin pie.

I can't buy him blue flannel shirts or wool socks.

I can't keep him warm, or safe.

As the world turned on its axle and the days grew shorter, I had to let each "I can't" go, lifted to the sky until the wind could catch it and whip it out of my fingers.

Good courage. Let it go.

Without affliction there would be no comfort.

—SPENCER'S JOURNAL, '99

Many coworkers donated their vacation time to me. That's real giving and I felt humbled by the graciousness of so many people around me. But after about six months the time ran out, so I jumped into a short-term disability plan carried by the hospital.

My doctor had known me for years through the hospital, but being healthy, we had not forged a doctor-patient relationship until now. She looked at me through her thick oval glasses perched on her nose with my thin record across her lap and made mention of my weight loss and lack of sleep. So she did what doctors do – she offered prescriptions.

No, I politely said. I had traveled that road to the end, during my Mt. Sinai psyche ward days in New York. I knew where antidepressants and sleeping pills led – nowhere. And in Nowhere, people don't get better; they just keep from blowing up. I believed God had more for me than that.

"I'm grieving," I told her, as we sat in the examining room, my records in her hand. "I don't need pills, just time."

"A little Prozac will help you to focus."

I smiled. The need to focus was on the bottom of my Wish List. "You watch," I told her. "A year from now, you put me next to someone who takes pills, and I'll come out better. Jesus will help me."

She smiled, and let out a small sigh, closing my folder. She was kind and being a physician, wanting to heal, to fix. We had to meet on occasion to satisfy the folks from the disability insurance company. They were already pestering me, and the conversation usually went like this.

"Mrs. Farnsworth, I see you are disabled but you are not taking any medications and you are not in therapy, is this correct?"

And I would say *This is true.* Then I would tell them a brief synopsis of why I could no longer be an ER nurse and they would be silent and sometimes sorry. Once I made someone cry.

"My pastor counsels me when I need it," I assured them.

God is helping me, I would say, and wait for an uncomfortable silence on the other end. Sometimes it even was a stretch for me to believe it, but I did. He was there, in every step, every breath. He had become my portion, my deliverer. And someday He would be my song.

9

THREE STARS, THREE HOOKS

Orion rises into the winter sky, sword lifted. I was in a habit now of perusing the sky often, as if Spence might duck out from behind a cloud or constellation and say,

Hey mom! I'm okay!

Seeing the three stars of Orion's belt makes me sigh. It's crazy I know, but Spencer had three small moles perfectly aligned across the right side of his face. It's like I'm seeing just a part of him a million miles away. People say, *Do you feel Spencer with you?* And I say, *Never.*

I don't think there's anything on earth to compare to heaven, except a rare taste, just a whisper of God's glory, like the day He came into my kitchen. I know the air is different there – and colors; can you imagine new colors? Music, beyond the greatest symphony or choir, way beyond. And even smell – intoxicating, rich and vibrant. Just one minute would kill us here on earth. That's why God hid Moses in the cleft of the rock. We can't see Him here and survive it. We are too small and dull, and terminally full of ourselves. In heaven we are different, like a bird released from a trap, and I'm glad. I'm glad it's nothing like this place.

I turn the last page of the Monet calendar Spence gave me for Christmas last year. I feel tired, weak.

> **JOURNAL 12/13/2002**
>
> *Jesus, draw me close to your side. Pull me near to you, where there are no distractions – just your glory, your love, no words, no Why's. Just you.*
>
> *Thought: God really does give us more than we can bear. But His strength is made perfect in our weakness.*

I did not even think of the three hooks set into the trim of the staircase in the living room. But as I passed by them daily, or sat on the couch staring numbly at the Christmas lights on the tree, my eyes invariably turned to the three hooks. Three hooks. Three Christmas stockings. But now only two sons. I had endured all the painful reminders of Spencer's loss and yet this one seemed unbearable.

The stockings themselves were unique, something I was proud of creating. You see, I don't sew. I dislike sewing so much I taught my sons how to sew so I didn't have to mend their clothes and replace their buttons. But the stockings were different.

Following my mother's tradition (and she was an excellent seamstress), each stocking was made of real red velvet and lined with green satin. But the best part was each stocking was decorated with something that pertained to each child.

Spencer's stocking, being the first child, was the most ornate. His dad was a fisherman at the time, so I made a boat with beaded sails and stars in the sky, then attached different symbols over time; a rocking horse from his second Christmas, a guitar with glittery musical notes above it. Each boy's stocking filled up over time as I introduced skateboards, basketballs, cowboy hats and drums using felt, beads and glitter. And each one was a labor of love, especially from someone who does not sew.

Three hooks, two children. I tried to ignore it. Then one day Jake said, "Hey mom, where's the stockings?" and Miles chimed in from another room, "Yeah mom, where *are* the stockings?"

I acted surprised like it had just been an oversight even though they had always been hung weeks beforehand. I retrieved the two stockings and hung them, my heart weary with loss. I knew it was a small thing but the red velvet stocking with the fishing boat on it had to go too. One more thing that should have been there but...

Sometimes grief is like a spinning room.

Sometimes grief is like a waiting room too.

January 2003

2nd Corinthians 12:9

The searing light of a new day
    The weight of pain settles evenly
Upon my mind, my heart, the body groans.
    "My grace is sufficient"
You should be there
    The familiar step, quiet
You were like the wind, sometimes
    Gentle, sometimes shaking the whole house,
Your heart filled with a greater love
    Than you could bear.
"My grace is sufficient…"
    Selfish I am, wanting my portion
That cup of contentment a mother
    Expects in her later years,
Drinking in the beauty of her child's
    Youth, stronger now than her
And able to return love for love.
    The chalice is snatched away.
"My grace is sufficient…"
    Here am I, now, strangely frail
Pride of strength or accomplishment
    Gone, and no prayer within me besides
"Oh Jesus help me."
    Your cup has become mine also, Your
Strength made perfect with each sip I take.
    "My grace is sufficient…"

10.

THE TRIAL

As near Thy cross a garden lay,
So, as we follow in the way,
We find a garden. Pain and loss
Were not the last words of the Cross.

– AMY CARMICHAEL, *MOUNTAIN BREEZES*

I went back to work. But I forgot how to be an ER nurse, and also realized that I really didn't have the right stuff anymore. I was skittish, easily jolted, and my mind went on tilt under stress. My heart would race and I had an almost uncontrollable urge to run, which would manifest with pacing, sometimes even hiding. My boss and co-workers were very kind, assigning me to the "Spa" as we called it, the Urgent Care section of the ER. It was the crayons and coloring books of emergency nursing.

The trial was set for March, but there were false starts and delays with lots of legalese that I had learned to trust Rob Welsh with. It had been more than a year that six young men had languished in the local county jail, waiting. The charges ranged from First Degree Murder with Home Invasion to Assault and Battery. Rob was careful to explain all of the

Whys and Whens but just like ER nursing, it didn't stick. Still I wanted to get it over with.

> **JOURNAL May 23rd**
> *Day at court. Looking into the darkness of a human heart – the horror, so black, beyond dark.*
> *Tonight I forgot which side of the road I'm supposed to drive on. I've been driving for 30 years.*

Finally, a date was set - June 2nd. As the time approached, I again left work, too distracted to even handle the Spa. My mom came up with her money belt on.

"The sky's the limit, Bird," but she said *sky* like *skah*, the fluid roll of her accent bringing a strange comfort to me. She found her seat in the store, watching me flip through racks of clothes like I was getting ready to start fifth grade.

Chuck Peterson was the main detective assigned to Spencer's case. I met with him and a state trooper over the winter after I had casually mentioned that one of the defendant's had called me from jail one night.

"It wasn't meant to happen like that," he had said over the phone.

"Like what?" I wanted to know, although I knew what he meant. It wasn't supposed to be Spencer, and probably not murder.

His voice broke.

"I'm so sorry," he said.

The Yarmouth police just had a new station built, a big upgrade from the small one story building I had visited a few times when the boys were riding their crime wave. I was asked to stop by one night, to talk. Chuck was hoping to get some new information for the case through the phone call, but the prisoner was very careful with his words.

"I thought you moved away," Chuck said. "It seemed like Spencer and Miles just dropped out of sight, so I thought they were gone. Then I saw Miles playing at a game at the high school."

I explained that Spence had changed, that God had changed him.

He sat back in his chair, rubbing his chin, like he just thought of something.

"Yes, we keep hearing that from people."

The Barnstable Superior courthouse was an impressive granite building set up on a hill with two cannons pointing out towards the bay. A plaque explained that the cannons had to be cemented closed to deter mischievous teenagers in the early 1900's from firing across the street on quiet Cape Cod nights. Three large wooden columns held up the front entrance, no longer used.

Around the back, it's congested on June 2nd 2003, as dozens of men and women enter – reporters, lawyers, potential jurors, families and onlookers.

The District Attorney was a retired cop. I never met him face to face, but on the phone, he sounded like a TV cop, maybe from Southie, tough like leather and a voice shredded from tobacco. He called me at home one night to see how I was doing with all of the delays.

"I'm praying for just two things," I told him, already knowing that a praying woman was a foolish woman in his mind. "For the truth to come out and for justice to be served." There was a pause, maybe even a low snicker.

"Those are nice things," he said. "But wait 'til you see what they do to it." I guess he meant nice things aren't allowed in court.

Upstairs Susan is watching for me, my family, any witnesses and Rob of course. I had given Rob a copy of Spencer's memorial video so that he could know him, the young man who would appear only in the last chapter of a very long night of January 25th 2002 into the first hours of the 26th.

"I've never seen him work on a case this hard," Chuck had confided months earlier.

I find Susan's office, "Victim-Witness Office" stamped across an old wooden door at the end of a hall outside the courtroom. Chairs and a couch line the walls with Susan's big messy desk in the midst. I take a seat on the couch and the steady flow begins; cops, state troopers, doctors, paramedics, scared kids with their mothers.

I learned Chuck likes history, likes to travel and loves to read. I learned that Rob Welsh was a fighter but fair, that behind the law is also what is right, and that God does hang out in courtrooms – beside the judge, in the witness stand, and within a broken mother. Then He walks next to the young murderer, feet shackled, and trying to look brave. Jesus is there in the midst of it all.

When you pass through the waters, I will be with you;
and through the rivers, they shall not overwhelm you; when
you walk through fire you shall not be burned, and
the flame shall not consume you.

– ISAIAH 43:2 ESV

It was hard seeing Zane. They decided to try him first, and try him alone. He looked a lot like I had remembered him in 7th and 8th grade when he was at my house all the time. He was funny and bright, with eyes that were kind but restless. He and Miles were best friends for a time, sharing a love for basketball and small trouble. Then Zane was cut from sports. I recall being at a middle school basketball game and a teacher yelling at him from the bleachers to get out, how all the parents glared at him in agreement even though they didn't know him, and I felt embarrassed for him and sickened by the teacher's performance.

Miles made the team barely. He was a great basketball player with a wise mouth and a quick temper. They were watching his every move. Several small arrests had landed him community service scraping barnacles off of the town docks. *Just like his brother,* some said.

As the two boys entered high school, Miles veered one way – towards sports and eventually college, taking a signal from Spence, who had just returned home from lock-up and was turning his life around. And Zane went the other way; dropping out of school, small trouble getting bigger.

I was struck by how handsome he was – well built, average height with caramel skin and dark eyes that were now looking away, but I remembered how they could be playful, yet sincere. He must've turned 20 after waiting in the county jail for this day. I had to look away.

The jurors were mostly women my age, mothers I imagined, and a few older men. They were all mixed in color. My brother Graham had driven up to sit with me for a few days when C.B. couldn't, and Peter, Spencer's dad, and his wife sat near by along with Aunt Patsy, an old friend from Jersey who loved the boys and stayed close through the whole trial.

When you pass through the waters…

Opening statements began. Each attorney told the story, the facts, facing the jury. There was a party, another party, a fight, and another fight. Retaliation, revenge. A cop is called. *What did you see?*

A door broken down. A window smashed. The frame in the yard.

A hallway. There was blood everywhere. And a man down, shallow breath. A girl holding a towel to his chest.

I will be with you…

Screams, chaos, Shawn, "It was Rodolfo and Myland. It was Zane."

A crowbar, a golf club broken in three, near his feet.

Whose feet, Officer?

Spencer MacLeod.

Shawn Kimball was called to the stand. You could tell Shawn had some military background – he stood straight and tall but he was nervous and his voice was erratic as he was battered by the defense attorney. He had not seen Spencer the whole night until he came rushing down the stairs as Shawn was being attacked.

Blood was gushing out of his chest as he tried to make it down the hall. Still he tried to ---it was real courageous what he did.

After the intruders left, Spencer got up and tried to make it to the kitchen, to the phone. He was softly talking, to no one anyone could see.

I tried to smile at Shawn, to let him know I was proud of him. You could tell he didn't want to cry, but his voice was breaking.

Spencer collapsed. Then another man who had hid in a bathroom upstairs, and Arheesha, Spencer's girlfriend, came down to attend to the wounded. Arheesha was a soft-spoken little girl, frail and thin who didn't look like she could keep upright in a strong wind. We met for the first time at the memorial service, and in time she would be able to tell me what my son's last minutes on earth were like. It's still a comfort to know that her sweet voice telling Spence how many people loved him, including God, was the last voice he heard.

"Every body thought we were fooling around when we'd take off but we would just talk – we talked about everything," she told me over the phone. "He told me he didn't want to touch me, to hurt me because he didn't know where he was going."

I smiled. He was hurt by old friends who teased him when he became a Christian and stopped chasing girls.

"One time he walked me to the door and I told him, 'If I'm your girl, can you at least just give me a kiss?' So he bent down and kissed me, just a little kiss."

Arheesha had moved to Georgia to be with her sister a few months after losing Spence, and now her voice had acquired a hint of a Georgia accent, causing the jurors to lean forward to hear. The room was packed; the back was lined with reporters and a steady ebb and flow of cops, but you could hear the old benches creak as people readjusted and shuffled their feet.

The defending attorney was a big man who looked like he had been raised in an Irish pub, but he was gentle with her. As she spoke, she looked my way often and I would nod and smile. I felt bad for everyone who had been pulled out of the normal rhythm of life, into a packed courtroom to answer questions about a murder. It had been almost a year and a half, but I knew for Arheesha it did not seem like a long time.

"I'll never find another man like Spencer," she had told me before she moved.

"Just look for a man who loves Jesus," I suggested, knowing it wasn't that easy, that her life was not gentle and sheltered and now this. I could see she was still reeling.

She got through the cross-examination, recounting my son's last minutes alive, and was gone. After a few more witnesses we broke for lunch. Across the street, in a small café, lawyers mixed with street people, ordering thick sandwiches on plates piled with fries. It was June; it was a perfect Cape Cod day, the kind where you can stretch out under the sun in the warm sand and breathe with the rhythm of the soft waves.

I sat at the table with Graham, Peter, and a few others, grateful Graham was trying to laugh and keep things light.

When you walk through the fire, you shall not be burned; the flame shall not consume you.

I could not eat, I wanted to but I could not. My chest hurt again. *Not again, Father.*

The laughter was loud, rising up over the tables, through the window into the pretty spring day. I had an urge to get up, and run and run, maybe to the cemetery, somewhere quiet, where truth lay still beneath the soft earth. I heard all I ever wanted to know, but still I only know one thing. You are not here Spencer, not with me, and I am alive, but gone.

Jermaine was a key player in more than one way. Yes, he was the guy Zane wanted to kill. But he had stepped out of that apartment just five minutes before the white Suburban pulled up, spotting Shawn Kimball through the kitchen window. Ten minutes later Jermaine returned to the apartment as the police pulled up. There lay his friend Spencer, taking his last breath, in a slick red puddle of his own blood, and Arheesia leaning over him as Shawn lay close by, alive, in shock and severely injured.

As the story unfolded, it was Jermaine who had provoked Zane into a murderous rage by holding him in a headlock so hard that in his own words Jermaine stated, "I thought I might break his neck." So he released him and left the party a second time, retribution paid for a previous fight, not knowing he would be tracked and hunted.

Julio was his real first name, and that's how he was called to the witness stand. He had put on some weight in a year and a half; a common phenomenon for young men coming off the streets into a warm church where food was central to fellowship. Pots of chili and plates of brownies rounded out the ex-drug addicts, softened the hard lines and gaunt faces. As Zane's lawyer shot questions at him, Jermaine answered in a low voice, stumbling a few times in his nervousness, recalling a night a year and a half before that he could never forget.

Then the strangest thing happened. Right towards the end of the cross-examination, the Defense Attorney said, "Now Mr. Concepcion, since January of 2002, you have experienced some type of conversion of sorts?"

"Yes, sir."

"Would you tell us briefly what that was?" Jermaine looked over at me and we both smiled, thinking the same thing. Go for it.

"On 2/2/02 I got saved by the blood of Jesus Christ, through his mother witnessing to me, through what the Bible says, and I gave my life to Christ."

The courtroom hushed. No one shifted, or even seemed to breathe, even the old grandfather clock waited, like time was suspended. I looked over to the jury box, and they were transfixed, each head turned to the witness stand. The judge watched Jermaine as he pushed ahead, describing his old life on the streets.

"I was an alcoholic, a womanizer and a total scumbag," he stated. "And you know what? I was full of pride. But Jesus Christ has set me free."

When he finished, the Defense Attorney took a moment to speak. I think some angels standing next to the judge were high-fiving each other. I wondered what possible good this could do for his case.

"Is that why you are telling us the truth now about what happened then?"

"No sir," Jermaine replied. "I told the truth back then."

The cross examination was brief, less than two minutes.

"And Spencer Macleod, when you leave to go to West Dennis for this retaliatory fight, says, 'Don't go.' "

"That's right, he said, 'Don't go'," Jermaine answered.

"And he didn't go?"

"He didn't go."

"And in fact, Spencer Macleod didn't participate in any fighting that evening, did he?"

"Not at all," Jermaine said, softer.

"That's all I have," Rob said, turning back to his desk.

When Spence was still at home, sometimes I would come in the door without him knowing and I would hear him praying in his room. He prayed a lot, on his knees over his bed, face into his pillow; sometimes it sounded desperate, like he was crying, his voice tormented. Sometimes he sounded like he was sitting on the throne next to Jesus, like he knew what he wanted was what God wanted too. On almost every page of his journals, there is a brief prayer list at the bottom. It is always of others; his brother Miles, his dad, and all of his old friends. The name that pops up most is Jermaine. Like he knew he was a key player too.

Spencer's Journal, 12/2/00

Only the present matters. Are you washed in the blood of the Lamb? Not, "were you washed." God loves you, even in our filthiness. Tomorrow is not promised. Embrace his love now.

Thought: Forget your past, all of it – good and bad.

Live or die for NOW.

The jury deliberated for two days. I could sense the stress on Rob, Susan and others that roamed the court hallways, making small talk. I tried to stay out of the way and took walks outside. Families of the defendant's stood in clusters; other groups included those who had testified, or were just there to rubberneck. Unless I initiated a conversation, I was pretty certain I would be left alone. Zane's mom approached me as I was heading back inside. She had been kind to me, but I avoided contact with her. It was too confusing and too deep.

"Robin," she stood before me, blocking my way back. "I really don't think Zane did this."

I stared at her, her eyes desperate and sincere. *She's just being a mom too.* Our loss was different but linked forever to January 26th, 2002. We were changed. And one way I had changed was I had no patience for social decorum or smudging the truth. Sometimes the outcome was blunt.

"Your son killed my son. I'm sorry but you need to let him face it like a man."

She searched my face, her expression unchanging and knew there was nothing more to say, so she stepped aside.

The jury was ready.

Murder is a very big deal. It took the judge two hours just to explain the law around it. There's First Degree, Second Degree, Felony Murder, Insanity Pleas. Then branches off of branches. It sounds complicated but it's not; it's just a lot to remember. Years ago, the judge said, the charge of murder was so respected that they would make the jury stand while they were instructed in the law. But now it takes too long.

Emotion can play a small part in the decision, that's why there were lots of moms in the jury, but the law demands fulfillment of specific criteria before you can convict. Zane's actions fit the requirements for First Degree Murder. As each juror stood and reported their vote, I heard sobbing from the other side of the courtroom where Zane's mom and sister sat. Peter wept softly beside me as the courtroom shifted and a low rumble moved like a wave across the room. Lawyers whispered across each other. Cops nodded silently, and reporters scribbled.

Zane stood, looking straight ahead, as he received the guilty verdict. He was 20 years old and he would live the rest of his life in prison.

Shawn stood first to read his Victim Impact statement. Poor Shawn. For years he would wonder if he could've done more, if it should have been him. He detailed his many injuries from that night which included emergency surgery on his bowel.

"Spencer is in heaven and I'm still here. Spencer was ready. I was not." His hands shook as he continued reading from the crumpled paper. "I am constantly sad and scared. I am making peace now with the Lord our God. I am getting ready."

After Shawn sat down, Rob nodded towards me. The courtroom was still filling as more cops and reporters squeezed into the back. Zane continued to stare straight ahead. I felt no anger or rage – instead a deep and weary sorrow that washed over me as I walked into the center of the room. Spence had seen Zane off and on over the years and was saddened by his direction, the same direction Spence was heading before God intercepted.

I began with my last night shift in the ER, then moved to who Spencer was. We had all just listened to the story around his death, for two weeks, from a cast of forensics, doctors, detectives, wide-eyed teenagers. But the actual man, Spencer MacLeod, had made only a brief cameo at the end.

The last part of my statement said this:

If Spencer could speak now, he would tell you to be a man now too, Zane. He would tell you that the toughest thing a man can do is admit he is wrong and take full responsibility for his actions. That real men can get down humbly on their knees and cry out to God and ask his forgiveness. A real man is a man who has been broken and stands in reverence before an Almighty God.

I have been a Christian for 15 years, but Spencer taught me and many others more about being Christ-like than anyone else. The true Christian must forgive, and I have asked God to help me forgive you. Forgiveness is not the same as saying it's okay, but by forgiving you, I release your soul into God's hands so that His will and not mine will be done. I pray for your soul; that even though you may be confined by prison walls for many years, that your soul could be set free to know God's love, grace and mercy through Jesus Christ; and that you may realize the same hope that Spencer was sure of when he breathed his last breath; hope of heaven, a place without violence or pain, where the Bible says God wipes away every tear.

My prayer has been for the truth to be revealed in this trial and for justice to be served. I will not rejoice in a guilty verdict, but I will be satisfied that justice within the state's legal system has been served. For some involved in this trial, there will be a sense of closure. For me, there is no closure. I will always be Spencer's mom. My pleasure comes when I pass through the gates of heaven into my son's arms. I commend you to take on your punishment like a man and stand accountable for this act of murder. And I commend your soul into the hands of God who is righteous and the final judge of us all. May you know His mercy and salvation.

I sat down and Rob addressed the Judge with these final words before they moved forward with the sentencing.

"I think that concludes the victim impact portion, Judge. Just on the issue of sentencing, the Court heard the case. And obviously it's a case of a young man that got murdered, that was trying to help out another individual. He truly died a hero trying to help another and got killed as a result."

I crossed the parking lot alone, or so I thought, when I noticed one of the court bailiffs trailing about 20 feet behind. I turned and smiled and he ducked his head, a little embarrassed. He was young, not much older than Spence would be, with a Marine cut, and big of course.

"We have to escort you to your car," he explained. "Just in case…"

"I'm not scared," I offered.

"I'm sure you're not!" He stepped closer and stopped in front of me, looking over his shoulder before he spoke.

"What you did back there…what you said about forgiving," he stopped and shook his head, then looked down at his feet. I thought he might cry so I spoke.

"It's not me, I can't take the credit. It's Jesus, it's just doing what's right."

He nodded his head, and looked back down for a moment, then started to back away.

"Thank you, ma'am. Are you sure you're okay?" He smiled, knowing the answer.

"Yes, I am. You have a good day!" And he turned, taking long strides back towards the Superior Courthouse of Barnstable.

11.

THE JOURNEY

This life is nothing more than a pilgrimage to heaven.
This journey is a journey of the heart.

— SPENCER'S JOURNAL '98

By the end of September, all six men had been convicted and sent away. I was able to face each one and say *I forgive you, Jesus loves you.* I was tired, and alone a lot, unsure of my response to simple things, tears triggered now by a host of places mentioned throughout the trial, and nightmares took on a more violent dimension. I traveled a lot, seeking asylum and distraction. Church outreaches took me to Texas and Nevada, then to a Navajo Reservation in Arizona. I ran to the mountains, to New York but it all had the same end, like Wily Coyote waving at me with his hand on the dynamite plunger. But nothing blew up; it all just looked the same, as if each magnificent scene was a cheap print. I longed for home – heaven-home.

"You're not considering suicide, are you?" my brother Bob asked one day. I laughed. *No,* I told him, I would not do that, and I meant it. Instead, I shouted at the sky, still searched the clouds, the stars, for my boy. I thought if I could just check on him, like when your kid has his first day of kindergarten and you know he'll be fine but maybe I'll just peek around the door and make sure...

Journal: Sept. 2, 2003

This I realize lately – that this road is only for me now, just fits one. Nobody can walk with me now; not C.B., not Graham, or Pastor Campo. It's only my road now – they just can't. And so, every morning I ask You to walk with me, Jesus, and You do. Funny that I don't ask anymore for a tangible sign. There's been no voice, no rainbow, no dove descending but YOU ARE THERE. Help me, direct me Lord, through these dark days. I am unsure of the next step.

Journal: Oct.16 2003

I realize I need to spend less time in this journal. Today I wrote cards to Rob Welsh and Susan O'Leary. I am turning the page. It is significant. Certainly there is no end to the pain and sorrow. Yet I am beginning to sense purpose. As long as I see you Lord, here with me on this planet, I can make it too. You are teaching me things – a lot lately.

Forgiveness

Forgiveness is a work of God. The world forgives but it is an incomplete work at best. Here is God's signature – not only the absence of hatred, anger and vengeance but also the actual presence of His love and compassion. Otherwise it is not true forgiveness.

Obedience

Obedience to Christ brings freedom. It's not only an act of trust in God but releasing our will to Him. We think it is our sacrifice but it is really His act of love to call us closer to Him.

Abandonment

I am finding that the very things I let go of in order to fully love Christ are some of the things He has given back to me, only with His perspective. When I stopped asking God "why" about Spencer's death and gained peace in just trusting Him, He has allowed me to see some of the "why," only from His perspective. I couldn't have seen it before – I wasn't close enough. I had to abandon first.

Courage

Someone said, "Courage is more than just grim determination." Real courage is also stepping out into His "fullness of joy," when all your sensibilities tell you to stop and hover at the edge of darkness, in the shadows of sorrow. I could live there always, and I'm quite sure that it is a place I will visit often.

I don't miss Spence any less or feel any less sadness that he's not here. But my eternal life seems to start where I want it to. I can wait until I die or I can meet God here, on this side, and ask for the "fullness of His joy;" His joy, strengthening me.

I still stand at the edge of darkness and weigh this out.

12.

SENT

Therefore, we are ambassadors for Christ,
God making his appeal through us.

– 2ND CORINTHIANS 5:20 ESV

C.B. hadn't slept at all in two days. Things just happened so fast. First a call to the pastor's office, then the question: *Will you take over a church?* It's a question we had wanted to hear since we were married. The idea of traveling to a foreign city, to shepherd a mish-mash of strangers, to bring the glorious news of salvation to a new place, even a new culture – we were all in. And the year before Spence died, our pastor had told us to be ready.

But it was a dream, along with others, that I had shelved in the shambles of my overturned life. I hadn't even thought about it, once, even though our church was a conference center for church planting.

"Pray about it," Pastor Campo advised us, "and let me know soon."

When we returned to his office to tell him we had decided *Yes*, he told us where we were going: Pawtucket, Rhode Island. To us, he could've said Honolulu, Hawaii. God does that for you, He just blinds you, then puts a deep, deep seed of love in your heart for whatever kind of place He puts you in.

Pastor Campo laid his huge hands on us and prayed – then we turned to leave.

"Pastor," I said, turning back at the door. "I'm not like the others, you know. I can't be like a normal pastor's wife." *Yikes, you sound really crazy*, I thought. But he smiled, and looked at me with compassion and some amusement too.

"You just be yourself, Rob. Just be who you are and you'll be fine."

I had only been to Pawtucket once when Spence was in Teen Challenge. They brought a van with speakers, music and mics into one of the projects there and set up on a basketball court. Spence rapped, others sang and Miles played basketball with a group of young boys while Jake played on the rusted out playground. One little girl took me on a tour, pointing out where everyone had died.

"Jimmy got shot right over there, in that doorway," she mentioned casually. She looked about nine. "And over there is where my cousin was stabbed." She waved her hand towards another tall brick building. We bought ice cream in someone's living room and headed back to the courts. That was six years ago.

We told Jake we were moving, leaving the only place he knew for somewhere none of us knew and he went upstairs and quietly cried. He was 11, in sixth grade and he was the most sought-after pitcher in Little League. But by the time we piled into the station wagon on Sunday morning and drove towards Rhode Island, he was excited.

It was November – it had snowed already but the snow was patchy and gray. The car rose up over a small bridge and there on the crest was a small sign that read *Pawtucket.* Someone had hit it, so it was crooked and looked like it had been stuck in a snow bank. On the other side of the bridge was a donut shop that sold Lotto tickets.

I never for one moment did not love this sad little city. There was something there that pulled me in, and I know we all felt it in that station wagon that day; my exhausted, nervous husband and a boy who had just left his world behind.

The church we were inheriting was a storefront church at the end of a small strip of stores, adjacent to a Chinese Restaurant. It was one large room with a small platform and a pulpit in front, a few dozen folding metal chairs and a tiny bathroom. Jake eyed a deserted drum set. Downstairs was a basement where we held children's church.

Downtown Pawtucket was a ghost town, now that Wal-Mart and the Emerald Square Mall had seduced the last customers of a once thriving city through their doors. Red brick mills were scattered along the Blackstone River and throughout the city, most of them empty. Some burnt down – "urban renewal" they would say with a snicker and a sideways look, the Rhode Island humor we grew to love. But there was a timeless beauty and majesty to the old crumbling structures set against the winter sky. In a deep snow you could imagine years gone by, of industry and prosperity, laughter and hope.

Pawtucket, also known as "the Bucket," was quiet for a city, sort of a shiftless *what-do-we-do-now* undercurrent in the way people walked or didn't. In the summer, folks hung out on the porches. In the winter they slipped inside little rooms thick with smoke. The kids in church would smell like fried drumsticks and ashtrays.

I think God is much like this: He walks along the dreary wastelands of this earth and imagines things. He looked at me all those years ago, beat up and worn from years of hushed pain, body and soul wearing thin and stretched almost to death. He saw something entirely different. I was angry and tired without knowing why but he saw something to salvage. I always thought he saw Pawtucket like that too.

Christmas came quickly our first year there. There was something so delightful in the garish decorations strung across dirty front porches and sagging balconies. The gray city seemed to come alive with blinking color, all inhibition set aside, like a sudden burst of hope. There was no restraint. Reindeer and Santa and baby Jesus all competed for the tiny patches of worn out lawns. Extravagant, like angels singing over some dirty shepherds.

I let the children in church decorate a little fake tree that was left there. We had no heat in our basement room except for a little space heater we would all huddle around with our coats on. They wrapped and adorned that tree with yards of tinsel and garland until it was nothing but glitz and glitter. Then we put lights on it and plugged it in. That cold damp room was transformed. I still see the little faces lit up, reflecting the bright tree. I think they knew without me telling them that the fake tree is like us and all the rest – the beauty, the light, the warmth – it's all like God's glory and He loves to pour it on. Then He likes to stand back and watch us trans-form, beauty for cold ashes, reflecting His very own glory.

We bought a hundred year old Dutch colonial in the cen-ter of town with more room than we needed. The boy next door was a Little League pitcher too and he and Jake talked back and forth at night with walkie-talkies because the houses were so close you could share house flies.

There was something about that house, with the high ceilings and the large front porch that helped me heal, like the mountains are for some people. Upstairs, the hallway had a tall window at the end that looked out across the rooftops of several multi-family homes, and at night as the sun sank beneath the angled skyline, the colors would splash into the hallway and it made me look up, like when you play in the surf and you are about to get hit by a wave.

And I remember one time, after we were there a few years, as I stood in the hall watching the colors shift into evening, the wave hit me, and I felt something strange and new – I felt joy. I forgot about joy completely, like a prisoner would forget about birthday cake or running through the waves at the beach. I did not hear a Hallelujah choir, but it wouldn't have been out of place. All I said was, *Thank you Jesus.* I was finally free.

Our soul is escaped as a bird out of the snare of the fowlers:
the snare is broken, and we are escaped.

– PSALM 124:7 KJV

13.

THE FOREVER BENCH

"Except a grain of wheat fall into the earth and die, it
abides alone; but if it dies it brings forth much fruit.

– JOHN 12:24 NKJV

Murder jolts three into changed lives

It was almost a full-page caption, with a large photo underneath of Jermaine, Murph and Brandon holding a framed picture of Spence. To the right was another article, *"His life touched so many people,"* with Spencer's face smiling from the middle of the page. That article began on the front page, an article about a memorial bench that was being dedicated to Spencer in a Yarmouth park. What made the dedication unique, the article explained, was that the Yarmouth police came up with the idea, and those that planned on attending included the Assistant DA as well as the Chief.

"This bench will be there forever," the Chief told Miles and me as we sat in his office. He was a good man, responsible in many ways for the integrity of Spencer's case. And when we met again to nail down some details to the memorial, a reporter was there as well. The Chief had a large envelope on the table and he slid it towards the reporter.

"You need to look at this," he said. "There's a lot more to this story."

Inside the envelope was a video I had given the Chief, called "One Year Later: The Spencer Macleod Story." A friend at church put it together, one year after Spencer's death, using pieces of his memorial video, woven into several testimonies of young people in our church who came to Christ as a result of Spencer's story. Most of them came off the streets or out of a lifestyle that was heading nowhere or to the grave. She looked intrigued. Before the meeting was over, I gave her a few names she could contact. Jermaine Concepcion, David Murphy and Brandon Gomes. They rented a house together and aspired to become preachers. I smiled at their faces, smiling back at me from the Cape Cod Times. She had found them.

"Spencer showed each of us about changing lives – that's the true product of Christianity, a changed life," says Gomes.

"Spencer's death brought us to the door, but Christ led us through," says Conception.

The bench dedication didn't happen until the fall. It ended up being two granite benches facing each other off the court, with a large granite stone in between. On the stone was a plaque that said:

Greater love hath no man than this,
that a man lay down his life for a friend.
John 15:13
In memory of Spencer T. MacLeod
1980-2002
And in honor of his courage
WALK IN LOVE

"Walk in love" is part of Ephesians 5:2, but more significantly, it was inscribed on my brother's gravestone, a verse from my mother's Common Book of Prayer that jumped out at her on the day he died.

The dedication fell on a blustery October day. It was a hodge-podge of the community: the Police Chief, the Fire Chief and several officers all in uniform, Detective Chuck Peterson, Assistant DA Rob Welsh with Susan, who handed me a dozen roses, my pastor, our families and many friends. The church served hot apple cider and baked goods while we took turns speaking, but I think I liked what Peter, Spencer's dad said most:

"Spencer was my hero long before he died. He became my hero when he gave his life to Jesus Christ."

Jermaine had formed a Christian rap band through the church, and they set up on the basketball court and did some songs, including one Spencer wrote. As the crowd huddled together, children climbed the rock with the plaque on it, and cops, ex drug addicts, detectives and once-thieves gathered together, leaves letting go from the trees, the north wind reminding us this might be the last of the beautiful fall days.

As the music and laughter lifted up through the pines and golden leaves, heaven was near that day, close enough to walk among God's children and hear Spencer's words:

This is a message to my heavenly Father,
Who picked me up when I was helpless, broken I needed shelter...
Though I walk through the valley of the shadow of death, I won't fear
Because Jesus promised that he would wipe away my tears
Never leave me, never departed
Because he's the healer of the broken-hearted.

14.

THE NEW MOM

After Spence died, my mother spun out into an orbit of paranoia and despair. She was sure we were all cursed. I think the real problem was she couldn't bear to think of me having to endure so much pain, because she knew, she knew so well. But I couldn't stand her company.

We'll take care of her, my brothers had said. After a few years, she settled down and gained some balance. Then I began to call her often, seeking guidance from her for the first time in my life.

You'll never like Christmas again, she told me once and I disagreed just because I didn't want her to be right. But she was.

In 2007, I called her the week before Mother's Day.

"I'm coming down this weekend," I told her, then added, "and I'm staying with you." Long silence. We always loved each other, usually liked each other but never understood each other.

"Okay, oh, that's great Bird!" Her voice was high and chipper. I didn't care, I felt God pressing me to do this.

When I arrived she was like a teenager throwing a slumber party. She had stocked the fridge with junk food and we sat up all night talking, eating and watching movies. In the morning, after coffee on her little porch I got ready to leave. As fun as it was, I knew it was a strain on her.

"Here Bird, I want you to have this," she said as I was grabbing my things. She held out a white envelope. "These are Kina's letters to me, when Tim died. Now they're for you." She was looking down, and I took the envelope from her, then sat down on the couch to read.

Kina had been her mother's friend, and she had one child, about my mother's age, a little girl named Betty. One Sunday afternoon, while her husband was trying to take a Sunday nap, Kina told six-year-old Betty to go out and play, suggesting maybe her friend across the street was home. Minutes later, their lives changed forever. Betty was struck by a car and killed right outside their home. In 1964, as my mother reeled under the same crushing grief when my brother Timmy died, Kina's words poured off the page and into her heart, bringing some measure of healing, then and throughout the years.

The letters were hammered out on a typewriter, dated August 1964.

When I wrote to you before, I had just heard and was inarticulate for I suffered for you. Well do I know the inner struggle.

Even the sounds in the street are different. You go through the normal process of speaking with friends, of making the necessary decisions, of picking up the routine demands of daily living – all without meaning somehow. You have become two persons – one on the surface and one underneath covering a suffering so deep only those who have walked along the same path can in any way comprehend.

After Betty's death for both of us life seemed without meaning – with periods of numbness then agony, with unanswerable questions pressing for an answer, with no haven of calmness or acceptance.

We went to Europe, and there in the dim, silent interior of the Cathedral of St. Denis, unknown parents spoke to us from across the centuries.

It was a small inconspicuous little bronze plaque near the bottom of the altar. The late afternoon sun shining through the stained glass window formed a shaft of soft blue light which centered on the small plaque, causing the inscription to stand out with arresting clarity. The words on that plaque have been engraved on my heart ever since, and have been a real comfort.

"For the years of our child's life, we thank thee Lord."

I stopped there, letting the ancient words settle, then felt the hand of God press them into my heart, like holding pressure to a wound.

We thank thee, Lord. For the life that began as a heartbeat next to mine, for watching the child become a beautiful man, for Spencer. Am I grateful? I thought probably not, but the question stayed poised in my mind, begging a truthful answer.

I folded the letters and carefully tucked them back into the yellowed envelope.

"Thanks mom."

Her hands were folded in her lap, and she suddenly released her fingers and slapped her knees.

"Well!" It was her cue for space, and I stood up. She hated goodbyes. Actually, she refused to say goodbye. When she came to visit us and it was time to go, she would get up in the dark and slip out the door. We would hear her engine start, and the car pull out.

"Why does she do that?" my husband asked once.

"What?" I never saw it as strange. It was just mom, her short cut around the clumsy mess of parting.

That morning, on her couch, we had finally found a common ground; two mothers, each had buried a son. Inside a pain and sorrow so complex was a place of familiarity between us that needed no explanation at all. And as Kina's typewritten words that were born from the depth of her own anguish and despair came alive with a flash of hope before me, I felt as if my mother's hands were gently holding me, how mothers do, and making things all right.

One week later, Bob called. Mom had had a stroke. A massive bleed in the left frontal lobe of her brain left her looking totally normal, but mentally devastated. Judgment and reasoning were gone. Once, she slipped out of a doctor's appointment, deciding to walk home in the 95-degree heat. Five miles later, she was found stumbling across the New York Interstate. A kind man picked her up and drove her to a nearby fire station where my brother was called.

We took her license, and moved her to an assisted living complex, walking distance, for real, to Graham's house. He told her he wouldn't let her in if she didn't have a cane with her, although she'd walk down the street swinging it, like Charlie Chaplin. She became content in the small apartment, meeting with her friend Tillie for tea and planning uprisings in the complex, like boycotting the canned vegetables. When she wanted to visit me, Bob would put her on the bus with a note in her hand like a school child and ask the bus driver to please watch her if she got off before Pawtucket.

We all agreed we liked the New Mom best. The left frontal lobe must store your fear also because she seemed to be free from her typical pattern of anxiety, aggression and withdrawal. The New Mom laughed a lot, hugged a lot and gave up arguing. New mom just liked to play.

September 2008

"Hey mom!" I scanned the ICU room and saw both of my brothers and one of my sister-in-laws encamped around my mother's bed. I had driven fast from Rhode Island when I got the call that mom had had another stroke, not knowing what to expect this time.

She had just recovered enough to adjust to her new life – no car, the tiny apartment and her grown kids meddling in all her business. Now, nearly a year and a half later, it happened again – this time on the right side of her brain.

As we sat in the ICU, trying to discern what this Newest Mom would look like, she smiled and wiggled her pointer finger at us like it was a puppet, then began to giggle. We laughed with her, relieved that she was happy. And for the most part, she stayed that way. The intellect that she was so proud of had completely vanished. *This* new mom was about three years old.

Mom had moved a lot since she sold "the big house" in Riverside in 1981. She would just get settled, then something she could never leave behind would start to prod her, making her edgy and restless. She stayed on the Cape for several years, then moved to Boston, then the Cape again, then North Carolina with my sister, then back to the Cape. Finally she ran off with Gordon, a mean man with a lot of money, giving all of her furniture and belongings away. She even gave me her Bible.

"I won't be needing this!" she said, and she was gone. Gordon was a total disaster. She traveled all over the world with him, like a whipped puppy dog. We all knew she was miserable, because he was. I can't remember ever seeing my mom lying in bed sick, but in one year she was laid low by pneumonia, shingles and finally breast cancer. Eventually, my brothers had to rescue her and set her up in New York near them, hoping she would find some peace, and to the best of her ability she did. She even started to like her grandchil-dren...most of them.

After the second stroke, we knew that the Newest Mom fell out of the Assisted Living parameters. They placed her in the "rehab" section of the complex like a broken toy not worth fix-ing anymore. Bob and I went to her apartment to pack her up.

The place was so small she had to buy a twin bed and a love seat in place of a couch. There was no kitchen, just a mini fridge and a microwave, which had become too confusing for her already damaged brain to configure. We threw her clothes into bags, and boxed some books she could no longer under-stand.

"I wonder what this is," Bob said as he reached up into her closet, retrieving a shoebox from a shelf. We put it on her bed and took the lid off.

We knew at once what it was, as we gently reached in and picked up a little boy's toy soldier, a First Place blue ribbon from a field day, an Indian Guide patch and a red velvet Christmas stocking lined with green satin. The trim and felt letters were hanging on with a few stitches of red thread, spelling "Timmy."

I remember it was one of those times where you can't speak. We were looking into our mom's heart, a place she kept even from herself for so many years. That this little box survived all of her moves, and the final cut of her last move, made perfect sense to us.

Years later, when even my face and name did not change her expression, I would whisper *Timmy* to her, just to see if everything was gone. Nothing. The house was swept clean. No wonder she was so happy.

15.

CANCER

(OR DON'T OPEN THE OVEN WITH A WIG ON)

October 2008

"I'm sure it's nothing, but with your family history, we need a biopsy," my doctor told me. An MRI had revealed a dark spot in my right breast that wasn't there six months earlier. A few days after the biopsy, my cell phone rang during my lunch break. I excused myself and went out into the hall.

"Hi, Robin? Yeah, can you talk? Or do you want to come to my office?" my doctor asked.

"Yeah, I'm here, just talk," I said.

"The biopsy came back positive." She paused. "You have breast cancer."

I felt annoyed. I don't have time for this. My mother had just moved in with us, temporarily, in hopes that some of her brain might return. Then there was the church, my job.

"Okay. So let's get moving. What's next?"

"I'll set you up with a surgeon. You'll probably just need a lumpectomy, maybe a little radiation." Sure. I hung up and looked out the window. Cancer. Interesting. I went back to the break room and tossed my lunch in the trash. Cancer.

The oncology department of Women and Infant's Hospital was in a large black cube-shaped building near the south end of Providence. Garbage whipped across the street, drawing my attention to the duplex apartments across from where I was parked. A busted door swung on one hinge in the wind, two small children played on the steps. It was December 9th – it was cold. Where were their parents?

I was early for my appointment, a chronic compulsion that I could thank my mother for. But it was good to sit – I had to think, to pray. God. What does all this mean? My oncologist would want an answer today. He was an intense man from the Middle East somewhere. He spoke fast, slinging survival rates alongside medications that were all foreign to me, then wrapped it up with a terse, "If the cancer comes back, you will die." He and the Tumor Board had recommended chemo. The cancer had spilled into just one lymph node. But maybe this was my ticket home? Maybe I should just refuse it all and leave it in God's hands, sort of like Russian roulette. If I live, fine, if not, that's okay too.

I reached for a devotional I kept in the glove compartment. December 9th – it just came to me then; the anniversary of my dad's death. Chemo back then was so gruesome many people just chose to die, but my dad fought so bravely. Spence had just been born and he wanted to be a grandpa, like he found his calling. He had been mailing silly little wind-up toys to us, frustrated at being anchored in New York for his treatment.

I remembered going to the beach with him in Connecticut, when Spence was just a few months old and he was supposed to stay out of the sun because of the chemo, but he wouldn't stop holding him, even as the sun crept over his umbrella. He just sat there, rocking him gently, as he cooed and babbled to his only grandchild he would ever hold, both of them smiling at each other.

Then I thought of my new granddaughter, Brooklynn. I was there, in the hospital, when she emerged from her mother, her pink body turning blue after struggling to breathe through some fluid left in her lungs. The nurses flung her on a table, suctioning and pumping until she wailed a beautiful cry, her little body strong and regaining the right color.

"Welcome to parenthood," I said softly to Miles as we stood looking down at his new daughter, a tiny IV running antibiotics into her arm, and electrodes stuck to her brand-new skin.

Life is frail, I mused, gazing at the child of my child. And something else was unfolding deep within my heart, something new I couldn't identify. Now I know. It was legacy – wanting to know this child and to be there so someday I could say,

"This is our story, Brooklynn. Look what God has done!" And she could carry the story, the family treasure, to her child. Someday.

Now she was just a few months old, and something had stirred, distant like angel music, and started to sing again. A Bible verse came to me:

But we have this treasure in earthen vessels, that the excellency of the power may be of God, and not of us. 2nd Corinthians 4:7

This earthen vessel is feeling pretty worn out, I thought.

How glorious it would be to go home, to run to Spence at the gates, to see Jesus smiling as we embraced.

You need to fight. The voice of the Lord was clear, interrupting my daydream and I sat up straighter.

*I put my spirit in you. It's my treasure. I need you **here.***

That the excellency of the power may be of God.

Oh. I felt a little ashamed for being so selfish. I thought of Brooklynn again, her little face under the shock of dark hair, her smile. I looked up into the winter sky that seemed to reflect the gray poverty of Providence. I remembered Spence saying, "Who will tell them if I don't? Who will pray for them if I don't?" The treasure.

Then my dad's face, the last time I saw him, wearing an Irish cap I had bought him to cover his hairless head, as he walked through the doors of Sloan-Kettering Memorial in New York City. He was going in for more chemo; drugs so toxic that the treatment could well kill him. He turned and smiled, tipped his hat, then walked briskly through the revolving doors. He weighed about 130 lbs., barely enough to keep his large frame covered with skin. *Okay, Lord, I'll fight.*

I pushed open my car door, and bracing against the icy wind, headed towards the oncology building with my answer.

Winter 2009

"C'mon, mom, take my hand."

I closed the gate to the chain link fence that surrounded our small yard, and we headed down the street. The sidewalk was uneven and missing in places and mom was prone to stumbling. We kept holding hands as we strolled down the block, pointing to trees, birds and children. Sometimes she would start a sentence and it would end somewhere far off. Or she would parrot.

"Hello, how are you?" someone would ask her, passing by.

"Hello, how are you?" Mom would say. Then they would stop and start a real conversation with her while I waited for her to continue copying everything they said.

"I'm fine. Cold out today!"

And she would say, "Fine. Cold out today!" mimicking their voice if it was distinctly high or had a heavy Pawtucket accent. I would just smile at their bewilderment, figuring the explanation would take too long, and tug on her hand to keep moving.

"Our mom's a retard," my brother Bob commented once.

We walked everyday, if I could. The chemo had a pattern of creeping up on me, and I would start to feel like I was walking through waist high mud. I tried to keep going, sometimes asking C.B. to take me to the place every doctor tells someone on chemo to stay away from – the mall, a simmering potpourri of pathogens.

Around the block took us about a half hour, because to mom, it was different every day. And when we reached the gate again, and I led her up the porch stairs into the house, she would look around with eyes of wonder and say, "Oh, this is just beautiful!"

Cancer meant absolutely nothing to her. Only once, when I was coming out of the bathroom after a shower, did she comment on my bald head.

"It's a little short, Bird, do you think?"

As people dropped off soup or called to check on me, mom stayed attentive but showed no interest in the conversation. I could not have had her there if she knew. Worry would have sent her spinning into panic, then the rage, then we would all be doomed. Instead, she was happy with us, grabbing Stella, my aging cat, and trying to swaddle her like a baby, feeding Rosie and my pug Charlie anything she could find, including a whole jar of grape jelly at 2:30 in the morning.

It was hard, sometimes painfully hard, caring for my mom like she was a child but still respecting her as my 80-year-old mother. And at times my patience reached beyond frustration and I'd have to walk away. But I learned a lot from her that winter. And I learned a lot about me; my limits, my frailties, my neediness too. It was often not pleasant to acknowledge. But there is mercy and grace, especially when we decide to love beyond measure, without return. In those places we find the end of ourselves and a return greater than we could ever give.

One night, when we were sitting close on the couch, watching *Babe* again, she reached over and touched my face ever so lightly with two fingers.

"You okay, Bird?" she asked, her mother brows furrowed in worry. I smiled and put her hand in mine.

"Yes, mom, I'm okay." She hesitated, watching my eyes like she used to when I was a teenager and telling a huge whopping lie. I held my breath. Then she nodded and turned back to the movie, something deep and unsettled now quiet again.

At night I would tuck her in, and look at the child-like expression on her face as she pulled the covers up to her chin, and I would know that I had made the right decision to keep her close by as I rode out the winter, my body brought down to its knees by the cure for my cancer. I remember crying out to God, about six months after Spencer died, at the end of my last bit of strength, realizing the road had just begun.

"Aren't I broken enough yet?" I yelled, tear-streaked face turned upwards to the silent heavens.

Now you are, He said. And I knew, looking at the light from the street play across my mother's wondrous expression, that brokenness is where God lives. It is love made perfect.

My husband and I pastored for five years. You learn a lot on the other side of the pulpit. You learn that people are really messy, faithless and sometimes stupid – just like sheep. But God puts a shepherd's heart in a pastor and his wife too, so you love them, needing nothing in return. You just pray they stay and *Grace* is the air you breathe. It made me remember a young woman full of arrogance and attitude that sat in the front row of a movie theater I called "church" in Wellfleet, and how my pastor would call me *Blessing*. I wrote them and thanked them, and they wrote back saying I made them cry; I think in a good way.

16.

WHAT DOES LOVE LOOK LIKE?

2012

The fountains from which love flows are in God, not in us. It is absurd to think that the love of God is naturally in our hearts, as a result of our own nature. His love is there only because it "has been poured out in our hearts by the Holy Spirit..."

OSWALD CHAMBERS – *MY UTMOST FOR HIS HIGHEST*

What does Love look like? God again, and the emphasis was on *look.* I knew what He was asking. I had been asked to speak on different occasions on the power of forgiveness, and I made it a point of saying that forgiveness isn't complete unless the love of God is in your heart. It was true – but like a lot of Christian formulas, it was meaningless without being able to walk it out.

Words sound grand, but they get tossed into the wind and are gone.

My heart had been magnificently spared, as if God Himself cupped it and hid it beneath His massive wing. I could truly say that I never had felt any rage, hatred or vengeance towards any of the people responsible for Spencer's death. I had met other "homicide survivors" and the impact of how devastated their lives were without the grace of God surrounding them left me humbled.

Several years ago, a friend called and asked me to come over. A woman had showed up at her church that morning with her two kids. They had made a suicide pact earlier and they were on their way into the woods to take their own lives when they walked past her storefront church and instead detoured inside. A mom, her daughter, who was around 20 and her 15-year-old son. Two years earlier, her 16-year-old son had been murdered over drug money. My friend had invited her over after church for tea.

I listened to her tragic story and tried to encourage her, to show her Jesus was there to love her and her kids but there was something terribly wrong – there was a vacuum in their souls. They were indifferent, even to death. The only spark left was a dull hatred that laced her speech when she spoke of the two young men who had murdered her son. The outrage and pain had chewed on them from the inside out, and they looked like the walking dead. I was staring into what I would be without being anchored in Jesus when the tsunami hit.

I was never great at Love. Mom said people were out to take from you, and my dad used to say it was a dog-eat-dog world. I was good at guarding. But this is the main thing I love about Jesus – it's never been about what I have or who I am. It's who *He* is, and what He has is a fountain of grace, an ocean of love. All I have to do is ask.

What does love look like? God knows the answer. The test was mine.

17.

THE VISIT

God's most powerful revelation is of His grace.

– SPENCER MACLEOD

Feb. 2, 2013

Jermaine was running late. He had forgotten his wallet and had to backtrack. He was pastoring a church in Providence now, so he didn't have far to drive. I sat in the prison parking lot and weighed my options. It was cold out, and I was nervous. Sitting in my car looking at my phone would be a poor way to kill time. I watched as yet another young woman ducked from her car with a toddler on her shoulder, still asleep from the trip, hurrying into the building.

The Lord is my shepherd....

What am I so afraid of? Well, it *was* a state prison, imposing in size, with a tall cement wall running around it, topped with barbed wire. It was obviously old. Small details, like a cupola on the main building, are never seen in modern design. I had just driven for several miles through undisturbed country that I was surprised to find so close to Boston. Rolling fields and thick woods, like out of Walden's Pond, lined the road. Then, coming around a curve…Norfolk MCI, the state's largest prison. But that's not what I'm most afraid of.

I was invited to meet with Dave Myland, one of the six men convicted in my son's murder, serving a second-degree murder sentence; life with a chance of parole after twenty years. It had been eleven years since Spence died, and ten years since I saw David last. After two days of paneling a jury, a plea bargain was negotiated. They had been charged with first-degree murder, and had just watched their friend get sent away for life, without parole. Second degree looked like the better choice.

I had faced these two men, Dave and Rodolfo, who now lived inside this prison, on an August day in the Superior Courthouse in 2003. I was still numb from Zane's trial as I read a quickly written Victim Impact Statement. I was surprised then to look up and see that they were both staring at me, and listening. I said I forgave them. I said God loved them. Then I cried as they were led away in cuffs.

Now, exactly eleven years from the day I buried my son, I had agreed to a request from David to meet him. Having Jermaine with me was part of the deal. As it turns out, that part worked out well. Jermaine and Dave had been talking on the phone and two weeks ago, I got a call from Jermaine. David had prayed with him over the phone. He wanted what we had, complete forgiveness, to know the grace of a loving Savior. He surrendered.

Yea though I walk through the valley of the shadow of death…

I got out of the car and walked towards the main entrance, following a woman in front of me with two little girls skipping behind her, about my granddaughters' ages. The sky seemed small and dull just over the walls, and it was cold, bitter cold.

Once inside, I stood in a large crowded room, feeling conspicuous, the white middle-aged lady with the deer-in-the-headlights look. A kind woman handed me a bright yellow form to fill out, with a pen. Windows lined the opposite wall where I could see prison officials shuffling papers behind thick plexi-glass and bars.

Your rod and your staff protect and comfort me.

Jermaine finally arrived and we still had a lot of time to talk as we waited to hear our number called. I'm not sure why everything that has to do with the government needs to take so long, but here there was no exception. As a large steel door slid open, we were finally pushed through and I took my cues from a little girl before me who had thrust out her bare arm to an expressionless female guard with a big rubber stamp.

The Lord is my shepherd; I have all that I need.

After being searched and moved through two more steel doors, I was surprised to be outside again, chilled without my coat, then led into another building, sort of octagonal shaped. Once inside I found myself in a huge open room that reminded me of a waiting room in a train station, loud and echo-y, with vending machines everywhere and kids with lots of energy. I was expecting something different, like a small smoky room with rigid chairs and tense guards, maybe speaking through phones like in the movies.

I shall fear no evil, for You are close beside me.

I watched Jermaine as he scanned the room, realizing I didn't really remember much about how David looked that one day years before. Jermaine smiled and I turned to see a young man in jeans and a gray sweatshirt walking towards us, first greeting Jermaine then turning to me. Dave was bigger than I remembered, and perhaps looking a bit older than thirty but his eyes were gentle and it was easy to take his hand. Then I reached up and gave him a hug because it just seemed like the right thing to do. We stood there smiling and a little awkward while David looked for seats.

Driving up there, I couldn't imagine what I'd say. There were things I didn't want to talk about and I wondered what any of us had to say but I knew there was no sense in arguing with God. Sitting there with these two young men, our conversation flowed naturally with a depth and openness that is rare in life, a sharing of hearts and hopes that was understood, an unspoken link between us. Not one of us would ever be the same after January 26th 2002. A prisoner, a pastor and a mother somehow connecting lives in a way that can only be orchestrated through the power of a loving God. Three sinners, equally precious to Jesus – forgiven, redeemed, restored.

I don't think God separates us on this level. The world does, the law does and that's how it has to be here. But He knows we are all desperate – prisoners and guards, judges and junkies. As the setting sun turned the chaotic din of the visiting room into a soft sepia hue, a guard shouted, "Visiting time is up! Say goodbye!"

Daddies kissed their little ones goodbye, girlfriends promised things in low voices and a few brave mothers, weary looking, hugged their sons and slowly moved towards the door. I was glad it was so simple and easy to love David, to want to embrace him and really pray for him. Jermaine and I walked out together to our cars, smiling, knowing that we were on holy ground, that God was again moving in unsearchable ways, glorious and mysterious.

I can't explain any of this very well, because God can do things in a human heart that are absolutely impossible left to our own. But as I drove the long way home that day, I knew I had again glimpsed a bit of heaven on earth, right in the middle of that prison. If you know Jesus this shouldn't surprise you.

He restores my soul.

The gray February sky stretched out before me over the highway, the clouds dark and almost obscuring the setting sun, allowing just a few rays to reach the frozen ground. I wasn't sure whether I would sing or cry. I decided to sing.

Surely goodness and unfailing love shall follow me all the days of my life.

*All scripture from Psalm 23, NLT.

18.

WALK IN LOVE

July 28ᵗʰ 2014

A lot of things had changed, especially the old neighborhood. The maple tree was gone, and every other landmark I could recall from our front yard was exchanged for toney landscaping; ornamental trees and gardens replaced the lawns where children played until dark on summer nights, the lightening bugs flickering above us.

Ada's hadn't changed much. It still needed paint and had years of bubble gum stuck to the porch and sidewalk leading up to it. But a yellowing newspaper article taped to the window declared what we already knew. Ada was gone. *Lord, she must've been 100,* I thought when I first saw it. A pale young woman with a tense expression dutifully manned the register but it was no longer Ada's, just another convenience store.

The graveyard had mostly remained the same, except for the missing climbing tree. It had been fifty years, so it's hard to remember when the beautiful dogwood tree came down, the tree that gave shade to the small grave. I looked for a trunk, a hole, but there was no tell tale sign that the tree had ever existed. Yet in our memory, the three siblings of the little boy that was buried there, we all remembered the climbing tree and the different view that two brothers, twelve and four and a sister age eight, had back then.

It would've looked odd to anyone who passed by to see three graying 50 to 60 something adults, sitting in a semi-circle in lawn chairs around a small modest plot. The years of neglect showed on the rough granite stone, slightly mossy, with dry grass surrounding it.

My mother had transported pachysandra from our front yard, under the maple tree, to the gravesite and it flourished there. Perched above the grave, I'd watch her hands move through the tendrils of ivy, like she was tucking Timmy in. Then we would play hide and seek between the gravestones around him. Dad would stand at the foot of the short grave with his hands in his pockets looking down without words while mom bent down, talking softly to the dirt. The ivy was gone too.

The brother that we all loved, that went off to camp one sunny July day and never returned, is still a puzzle to us after all these years, like a question that can't get a good answer. And as we talked, the pain surrounding his death resurfaced, but after fifty years, it was less traumatic and more like an old friend we all knew, each in a different way.

It was Graham's idea – a sibling reunion on the 50th anniversary of Tim's death.

And now, fifty years down the road, as I sat between my brothers in a cemetery, that day was still so vivid; Bob running to my mom to be held, and Graham and me sitting side by side on the front porch step, looking up. We are still looking up. God hears, and He bends His face down to ours to listen. And if you wait, He will speak.

Before we left the graveyard, Bob looked down at the small stone and commented on the scripture engraved under Timmy's name: **Walk in love.**

"I think that's what really saved us," he said softly. "It was more of a command and it was the only thing we knew to do."

Any child can survive. So can any adult. But there is so much more than that. There is learning to love again, and that takes courage.

Cemeteries seem like a strange place for an awakening. Sometimes I would go down to Woodside Cemetery three times a day after Spence died and just walk over to his grave and stand there, reading the name and then the two dates beneath it, over and over and over as if I was memorizing a complicated formula. It made no sense. My heart was colliding with a truth I could not bear. So I planted things there, just to make something grow, and thought of the pachysandra my mom had planted so long ago.

There wasn't much to the Woodside cemetery back in 2002. It was January when I first stood there alone. The wind coming off the pond whipped across the barren hill leading up to the older graves. There were a few headstones scattered just above where I stood but the field around me was fairly empty. Just one grave with a woman my age buried beneath. Her inscription read, "Don't cry for me, I did not die… I live with the risen Lord!" I liked that and thought this might be a good place to bury my son, my child. It was one of those out-of-body moments when you know you are where you are, but you also deny it. I was cold, but it didn't matter.

Then out of the corner of my eye, I caught something moving up on the hill. Was it an animal? Someone watching me? I walked up the hill towards a more populated area of the graveyard and noted a large black stone with small trinkets lining the foundation. The large object that caught my attention was an enormous stuffed Winnie-the-Pooh, waving in the breeze, tied to a bush beside the grave.

As my eyes traced the name and the two dates beneath it, my heart sank. *Bruno...* born 1998, died 2000. He was clearly Brazilian and there was an image of a smiling little boy etched onto the stone, and then this scripture:

> *He who dwells in the secret place of the Most High*
> *shall abide under the shadow of the Almighty.*
> *Psalm 91:1*

It was familiar to me, but then it felt like I was reading it for the first time. I stood there for a while, gazing at the stone, the words, knowing that God was trying to work something into me.

I would visit that little grave often. Pooh Bear endured some snow and rain and I believe dried out periodically in the summer sun. Then after what seemed a long time, he disappeared but I could tell someone came there a lot, leaving small toys, little boy keepsakes.

I hadn't thought much about little Bruno until an early spring evening when I went up to the cemetery with Rosie. I could hear laughter and words in a foreign language drifting down the hill, and I spotted a little boy running among the stones, making airplane noises and the universal boy language of machine gun spray and crashes.

I flashed back to my own childhood, running and ducking behind the granite markers with my brothers, while my parents tended to Timmy's plot. I didn't want Rosie to crash a special time for this family so I stayed far away. Later I saw them walk down the hill towards the pond together, their laughter light and easy and they were holding the boy's hands as he skipped between them.

Curious, I walked up the hill to Bruno's grave. Fresh stone glistened in the evening sun and little ceramic frogs and lizards lay across the white gravel. Over to the right, a shiny ceramic Pooh bear smiled at the reptiles. Then I noticed the date. Born March 19th. Today was his birthday. How well I understood the significance, the sorrow that settles in a parent's heart, the silent nod towards a date that once brought such joy. But I thought of the little boy, Bruno's new brother, of the parents' laughter and their hands holding each other.

He who dwells in the secret place of the most high....

It was clear they had weathered the storm a lot better than that old Pooh bear. They had found the same secret place that God was ushering me towards on that cold January day as I was choosing a place to bury my son.

He is a Redeemer.

I walked back down the hill. The crocuses had pushed through the frozen earth; purple and gold bonnets seemed to call to each other across the gravestones and I noticed a few shy buds had appeared on the tips of the brittle gray trees. The wind came up from the pond, soft and damp as I made my way back to Spencer's grave. A thick blanket of vinca covered the earth where there once was a large hole, and from the tangle of green vine I saw just one purple flower, it's petals unfurled in the breeze.

My eyes automatically lifted to the stone and scanned the name, his birthday and his last day. Then the familiar verse:

"Well done good and faithful servant – enter into the joy of the Lord."

Well done, Spence. I can see him bursting through the gates, God's glory breaking over him like when he used to run full bore into the wild ocean waves on Edisto. Home. Joy at last.

Then I did something I had never done before. I bent down and touched the little crocus, smiling. It was not as fragile as I thought. *Brave flower,* I mused. Rosie watched me stand and turn to go, then ran to the car to meet me.

...shall abide under the shadow of the Almighty.

THE END

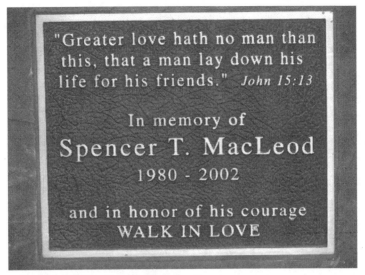

"Greater love hath no man than this, that a man lay down his life for his friends." *John 15:13*

In memory of
Spencer T. MacLeod
1980 - 2002

and in honor of his courage
WALK IN LOVE

Memorial at Old Town House Park in Yarmouth.

Me and my sweetheart, C.B. Farnsworth

Mom and me, after her second stroke and my chemo.

Miles and Erin with Brooklynn holding Quincy Spencer and Olive, 2017

Jake and Kayla holding Leo and Eli with dad, 2017

Left to right: My bros! Graham, me and Bob 2016.

The Visit: with Dave Myland (center) and Jermaine, Norfolk Prison

Rosie the Rescue Dog, 2002-2015

EPILOGUE

The highway to heaven is through our hearts.
We're going to appear before God.
This is the victor's path.

– SPENCER'S JOURNAL – '98

Several of the young men that surrendered to Christ through Spencer's testimony became pastors, plowing into the hard ground of distant cities, gleaning a harvest of souls. Many more can be counted as the Lord's through the ripple that spilled outward from an imperfect young man's life and death towards others, who then reached out to others, who reached out again. I can sit in my church and count whole families, abounding in love and fruitfulness, that would not exist but for Spencer's sacrifice. And this all counts, and I know there's more. Just this past month, six teens raised their hands for salvation at a basketball tournament held every year in Spencer's honor.

But to me, the greater weight lies beneath the numbers, within the hearts of so many who will never be the same. One night at work a few years ago, a secretary sat with me at dinner, a woman who had been in the ER the night Spencer was brought in. She brought it up carefully, and I smiled, giving her permission to talk.

"I have never been the same," she said, laying down her fork. "I wanted to tell you this for years. That changed me."

She began to cry softly. "It drew me to God, to where I needed to be."

It was not just how my son died, but how he lived. A young man who grew up with my sons and later began an intense battle with schizophrenia called me last Mothers Day. "I don't know if I ever told you this, but who Spencer was and his love for God changed my life. I started to really read the Bible after he died. That saved me."

I suspect it is what I can't see that means the most. How so many lives that were broken, just like Spencer's and mine too, surrendered completely into the hands of a loving Savior, discovering joyfully that our lives are not our own. We are His. Jesus is not an attachment; He is our breath, our life and our song. This is just one of His stories – sometimes sad, sometimes messy but with an astounding and somewhat mysterious beauty that is eternal. And He will use it over and over again, when we open our hearts all the way. No door, wide open.

> "It is not the level of our spirituality that we can depend on. It is God and nothing less than God, for the work is God's, and the call is God's and everything is summoned by Him and to His purposes, the whole scene, the whole mess, the whole package – our bravery and our cowardice, our love and our selfishness, our strengths and our weaknesses." – Elisabeth Elliot, *Through the Gates of Splendor*

2017

I am often asked to speak, to tell the Story, forgetting that what has just become a part of me, woven into the fabric of my soul, is peculiar and fascinating to most. It has all the parts that make a whole; conflict, searching, tragedy, resolution. And it seems that the good guy wins. But as Elisabeth Elliot cautioned at the end of her captivating story chronicling the martyrdom of her husband and four other missionaries,

"Cause and effect are in God's hands. Is it not the part of faith to simply let them rest there? I dethrone Him in my heart if I demand that He act in ways that satisfy my idea of justice."

This story has no end for me. In fact, just this year there was a segment aired on Boston's Chronicle about a mother who forgave her son's killer. David Myland and I were both interviewed; Dave from prison, me in my backyard. It seems like no big deal to me – you just forgive because God says to. It's certainly not my idea. It was just my response. But it is riveting to the public. She did *what?*

When I'm asked to speak, which is usually on or around the topic of forgiveness, people will invariably make their way towards me at the end and ask,

"What about (fill in the blank)?" They want to know how the story ends.

So for those who are curious, here are a few of the cast. They, like me, are ever changing and ever-growing each day, with a will that may swerve in and out of God's, but somehow I know that each of us are held securely in His everlasting arms – Jesus, the Author and the Finisher of our faith. (Hebrews 12:2).

- Miles: met Erin in college. She and Jesus chased him around the world. They married and have three amazing children; Brooklynn, Olive and Quincy Spencer. Currently living in Wake Forest, NC where he teaches English, Global Leadership and travels to Ghana with Erin every two years with a bunch of students. They both fervently serve God at the Summit Church.

- Jake: was shipped off to Jacksonville, NC from Pawtucket at age 16 to a sister church there and a wonderful family who loved him and prayed for him and fed him too. Met Kayla when they were kids but really noticed her after he gave his life to Jesus at age 17. Married after finishing nursing school and they currently have two beautiful little boys, Eli and Leo. Jakes works as an RN and they both serve God joyfully at the Door Christian Fellowship Church.

- C.B.: What can I say about a man who still loves me through all of this? He is a rock, but he has also become my best friend. We returned to our church on Cape Cod after my cancer treatment was complete. He ministers in prison every week besides serving in children's church. We celebrate 20 years together in the fall. Last year I gave him a card that says: "Marriage means commitment...of course so does insanity." Still crazy about this man!

- Jermaine: pastored in Providence, Rhode Island. Married with a bunch of beautiful kids. Still a soul on fire.

- Shawn: Suffered for years with the events of the attack, survivor's guilt, PTSD. He has had a fair share of trouble! But every now and then I see him in church, smiling, trying. Jesus never fails, never stops loving us. Keep going Shawn!

Six men convicted: Two released with lesser sentences, four still serving time, one for life. Two that I currently communicate with –

- Zane: Serving life without parole. Has expressed deep remorse to me personally. We are arranging a meeting in the fall. I pray always he will know the redeeming love and forgiveness that comes from Christ alone.

- David: Serving life with a chance of parole after 20 years. We talk occasionally; write occasionally and I've visited a few times. Recently our story and "unlikely friendship" appeared on Boston TV's *Chronicle* during a program on Restorative Justice.

- Mom: amazingly still alive. She is 88, lives in a small nursing home run by the Daughters of the British Empire, in an old Victorian home overlooking the Hudson in New York. She stopped recognizing me in 2011, my brothers, who live nearby, in 2014. Most days you can find her in a wheel chair, next to a big window, swaddling a baby doll then bringing it up to her shoulder to rock. She speaks no more, but still laughs easily.

- Detective Chuck Peterson: Retired recently to Florida, but returns twice a year to teach, using Spencer's case within his curriculum to "honor his memory." A friend and support to me and my family throughout the years.

- Assistant DA Robert Welsh lll: Promoted to Judge several years ago. An answer to prayer – that Spencer's trial would be run with integrity and that he would be remembered as a hero. A dear friend.

- Susan O'Leary: Recently retired as Director of the Victim Witness office at Barnstable Superior Court. I can't imagine anyone being better at a very difficult job. A friend always.

- Rosie the Rescue Dog: Put her down October 2015. She was deaf, almost blind and finally unable to take walks. A friend in ways no one else could be for almost 14 years. Not sure if dogs go to heaven but I like to think so.

Our Hope
By Spencer MacLeod

Our hope is what is hidden
Not seen with the human eye,
Is promised to the forgiven
From a God who does not lie.
We hope for what we do not see
This gives us hope in itself.
The present cannot dictate
What lies beyond our death.
So we will not grow weary
When all we had is lost.
Our treasure cannot be worked for,
Only Jesus paid its cost.
So when vanity and emptiness
Overwhelm us with despair,
We praise God for His promises
With hands raised in the air.

*"Set your hope fully on the grace to be given to
you when Jesus Christ is revealed."*

– 1 PETER 1:2

*** Found in a notebook of Spencer's after he died

ACKNOWLEDGMENTS

A special thanks to my brother Bob, for being my Writer's Group and fan club. And to my sons, Miles and Jake. Miles, my English teacher son, for correcting this really long paper and to both, for reminding me, when I needed it, of why I write, for pointing me to the "eternal weight of glory."

BIBLIOGRAPHY

Carmichael, Amy. *Toward Jerusalem.* Fort Washington, Pennsylvania: Christian Literature

Crusade, 1997

Chambers, Oswald, and James Reimann. *My Utmost for His Highest: Selections for Every Day.*

Grand Rapids, MI: Discovery House, 1995. Print.

Elliot, Elisabeth. *Through Gates of Splendor.* Peabody, MA: Hendrickson Marketing, 2015. Print.

Hession, Roy. *The Calvary Road.* CLC Ministries, 2004

Lewis, C. S. *A Grief Observed.* London: CrossReach Publications, 2016. Print.

AUTHOR BIO

Robin Farnsworth lives on Cape Cod with her husband, Calvin. A writer, speaker, and registered nurse, Robin also runs Higher Ground, a Christian ministry for incarcerated women. She loves visiting her two sons, two daughters-in-law, and five grandchildren, all of whom live in North Carolina.

spencersmom.com

98545998R00164

Made in the USA
Columbia, SC
01 July 2018